A Future in Five Minutes

A FUTURE
IN FIVE MINUTES

A biography of

Jacqueline Hill

Louise Bremner

fantom
publishing

First published in 2020 by Fantom Publishing, an imprint of Fantom Films
www.fantompublishing.co.uk

A catalogue record for this book is available from the British Library.

Hardback edition ISBN: 978-1-78196-341-8

Typeset by Phil Reynolds Media Services, Leamington Spa
Printed and bound by CPI Group (UK) Ltd, Croydon, CR0 4YY

Contents

ACTRESSES WORK LONG HOURS in repertory, hoping, hoping to be noticed. They reach the West End, the stars in their grasp. And disappointment comes when the play ends after a brief run.

Then, for the want of something to do, they appear on television to be seen by millions who cannot help and a few who can.

The few watched Jacqueline Hill. And they took action.

In five minutes television had created a future.

Evening Standard, 22 June 1953

Foreword

I KNEW JACQUELINE HILL as Jackie. My mother, Ann Davies, had worked with her on *Doctor Who*, and they became lifelong friends. I was about six months old when she moved into the house opposite my family's in West London with her husband Alvin and daughter Sasha, later to be joined by their son John.

I spent my whole school career with Sasha from nursery to A-levels, so Mum and Jackie shared the school run up until secondary school when Sasha and I got the Tube. Jackie was always glamorous, even first thing in the morning: her hair blow-dried elegantly from her face, her clothes always immaculate and on trend. She had an energy which as a child I found both inspirational and a bit intimidating! She wanted the best for her children, and her drive and ambitions for them definitely rubbed off on me. My Mum told me that Jackie's brother had been given the chance to have a further education, but that Jackie had been expected to go out and earn a living from the age of fourteen. Even as a young girl I thought that was a terrible and unfair way to treat a young woman. No wonder she wanted the best for her children. It also made me aware of the importance of feminism from an early age!

Jackie died when I was about twenty-five. She had been very ill with cancer. I remember driving her back from the hospital one day, knowing she was close to death. But she still had her hair elegantly blow-dried and her clothes immaculately presented. I admired that so much.

Jackie made a big impression on me as both a child and a young adult. She was a beautiful, talented woman who had tried her best to fulfil her dreams and wanted that to be passed on to Sasha and John. Jackie taught me, deliberately or without meaning to, the importance of being in charge of your own destiny. Especially as a woman. For that I am always very grateful to her. I'm also delighted this book has been written to celebrate her life. She would have been thrilled.

Lucy Briers
January 2020

Prologue

A T MID-MORNING ON THURSDAY 7 August 1930, twenty-four-year-old William Roberts went out to visit a neighbour. He left his father, Morris, at home with a woman called Mrs Robbins, who had come in to help them with the housekeeping.

Half an hour later, Morris announced he was going into the village to buy vegetables. Taking his packet of Woodbines, he stepped outside onto Dale Road. It was around eleven o'clock, cool and showery, with the possibility of thunder in the air.

Morris was fifty-nine and the father of at least eight children, ranging in age from twenty-four to seven. Their family home was a small red-brick terraced house in the Bournbrook district of Selly Oak, Birmingham, a neighbourhood of working-class housing mixed with light industry. His wife, Alice, had recently left with another man after many years of coping with Morris's alcoholism and violent abuse; around the same time, he had been laid off from his job at the Ariel motorcycle factory. This meant that, among other things, he could no longer afford to drink.

In early July he had swallowed a quantity of Lysol and placed his head in the gas oven, only to be discovered by his seven-year-old daughter on her return from school. After a spell of twelve days in Selly Oak Hospital he was discharged, but his mental health remained poor. He was maudlin and filled with regret about his treatment of Alice and the children. William, their eldest son and an ex-soldier, had come home to keep an eye on the situation, fearing for the safety of his siblings. As well as threatening to take his own life, Morris had recently begun to make alarming remarks about 'doing us all in'.

Morris walked north for about twenty minutes until he reached Pritchatts Road, where he climbed over a fence and made his way down a steep embankment towards the London, Midland and Scottish railway line. His boots left clear imprints in the cinder dirt as he crossed under the road bridge and approached the track.

Just before midday, William came back from the neighbour's house to find Morris no longer at home. Mrs Robbins explained about the vegetables, but William, alert to any sign of trouble, noticed that his father's wallet and purse were still on the kitchen shelf.

He left immediately for Selly Oak Police Station to report Morris missing. While he was there, a message came in: LMS railway inspector Joseph Houghton had spotted a body lying beside the line, with its severed head a few feet away.

'I suspected that this would be deceased,' reads William's statement to the coroner's inquest that followed. 'I went to the railway and walked to Pritchatts Road Bridge, where I identified deceased's body.' The inquest determined that Morris had been run over by the 11:27 New Street to Redditch train, and recorded a verdict of suicide while of unsound mind.

1

'We drove up to Birmingham, because she wanted to show me the street where she lived. I remember sitting in the car – it was pretty early in our relationship – and she thought she recognised somebody in the street. I remember her sliding down in the seat. She didn't want to talk.'

– Alvin Rakoff

B Y THE MID-1950S, when she and her partner took a drive through her old Selly Oak neighbourhood, Jacqueline Hill was a Londoner. She was living in a Notting Hill flat, working as an actor and model and spending her time with a circle of friends in the same business. Since leaving home a few years earlier she had worked hard to distance herself from her former life, and the last thing she wanted was to go back; but her feelings about this place were complicated. It still mattered enough that she needed to show it, if only briefly, to the person she loved.

Jacqueline was born at home on 17 December 1929. Her parents, Grace and Arthur Hill, were factory workers; Grace was twenty and Arthur twenty-four, and they had been married just over a year. They named their new daughter Grace Jacqueline, and called her by her middle name from an early age.

The Hills lived on Unity Place in Bournbrook, a narrow terrace of 'back houses' closely set behind the larger Dawlish Road. The properties were small and basic with shared outdoor plumbing, and many of the family's near neighbours were Arthur's relatives: his mother, stepfather and assorted uncles, aunts and cousins lived in the same tight cluster of homes. The house where Grace had grown up, over on Dale Road, was only ten minutes' walk away, but things were tense there that winter between her parents, Alice and Morris Roberts. Sometimes that tension erupted into violence. It wasn't an ideal place to visit with a new baby.

By the time her father killed himself the following August, Grace was several months pregnant with her second child. Arthur Jr. was born in January 1931. A snapshot from early childhood shows the siblings side by side: Jacqueline with a dark, shiny bob and a wide smile, Arthur half a head smaller, fair-haired and laughing in the sunshine.

Following Morris's death, Alice Roberts returned to Dale Road to look after their younger children. At some point afterwards, Grace too went back there to live with her mother, and perhaps to help support the household – although according to the Hill family narrative, when she first left Unity Place it was to run away with a lover. Both versions may be true, but what's certain is that when Grace moved out, Jacqueline and Arthur junior remained behind with their father, and they did not really understand where she had gone.

It was the beginning of a separation that would eventually harden into complete estrangement. Later, relatives on their father's side would occasionally throw the children scraps of information: Grace had been 'a bit of a thespian', and the man she had left with had worked 'in the roadshow business'. She had visited irregularly but often failed to turn up, and after a while her relationship with them had simply tailed off. Nobody went into detail about her chaotic family background, and the implication was that she could not be contacted.

Various records suggest, though, that Grace lived on Dale Road with her mother for several years in the mid-1930s. Rather than being out on the road chasing dreams of stardom, she could usually be found working at the same local factory as her estranged husband. The two of them saw each other regularly, even as she faded from their children's memories.

Grace may have believed the children were really better off not knowing where she was. Life on Dale Road had never been stable, and they were with their father in the home they had always known. But to Jacqueline and her brother, her absence felt like abandonment. It hurt both of them deeply, and would have a lasting impact.

This uneasy situation continued until late 1937, when Jacqueline was seven years old and her brother six. One Saturday evening in September Arthur senior, a keen cyclist, announced he would be going out on his tandem the following day. Sunday morning arrived and he set off, leaving the children with their grandmother. At some point he met up with a Bournbrook neighbour, Mrs Florence Hodgkiss.

Arthur spent several hours out cycling before heading towards home in the afternoon with Florence on the back of his tandem. According to a report in the *County Express* they were ten miles away to the west, travelling along Broome Lane towards the village of Clent, when they reached a crossing with the main Worcester to Stourbridge road. Here, whether through distraction or misjudgement, they overlooked a number of warning signs and road markings and cycled directly out onto the crossing. They did not notice a Midland Red bus approaching from the Worcester side.

> The 'bus driver, Herbert Crampton, of 8, Ernest Road, Dudley, said he was driving towards Stourbridge at about 20 to 25 miles an hour, and the first time he saw the tandem was when he was four to six yards from the crossing. It appeared to be coming right over the crossing in front of him, and an accident was inevitable. He sounded his horn, braked, and swerved, but the near front of the 'bus struck the cycle.

The bus drove over Arthur, breaking his leg and several ribs and crushing his internal organs. He died before a doctor could reach the scene. Florence was badly injured but recovered sufficiently to give evidence at the inquest weeks later, although she had to be helped to the witness box. The verdict was accidental death, with the coroner describing Arthur and Florence as having 'taken their lives in their hands' by disregarding the road signs.

Both Grace Hill and Arthur's mother, Sarah Brown, appeared at the inquest and gave statements.

> Mrs Grace Maud Hill, 80 Dale Road, Selly Oak, said that deceased was her husband. She saw him daily at work, and his hearing and sight were good. She was not in a position to say how he had proposed to spend Sunday afternoon.

Sarah Brown, 6, back of 145, Dawlish Road, Hill's mother, said she saw her son on the Saturday night before he was killed, and he appeared to be in his usual state of health.

Despite the size of Jacqueline and Arthur's extended family, nobody could agree on who should care for them, and for a time they were on parish relief. Eventually it was decided that Sarah and her husband Albert, their step-grandfather, would informally adopt them in partnership with their great-aunt Rhoda, who worked at Cadbury's nearby Bournville chocolate factory. There was a loose arrangement for their mother to visit, but this did not last. When Grace married one of her factory colleagues seven months later, Jacqueline and Arthur were told nothing about it, and they had little if any contact with their grandmother Alice or the other Roberts relatives.

Grace continued to work as a lathe operator during the war. In 1948, aged thirty-eight, she died of tuberculosis in Birmingham's West Heath sanatorium. By that point her children were teenagers, old enough at least to understand the complexity of the situation – even so, nobody informed them.

Later in life Jacqueline could remember her mother only as 'a sort of vague apparition, a shadowy figure'. She and Arthur found it difficult to separate genuine memories from imagined ones shaped by family discussion. There were so many unanswered questions: where exactly had their mother disappeared to? Hadn't she cared about them, missed them? Had she intended to come back one day? Was there some reason she couldn't?

Speculation was all they had. For all Jacqueline knew as she was growing up, Grace could have been sitting in the audience of one of her early amateur theatre productions – maybe even, later on, watching as she made her first appearance on television.

Decades later, great-aunt Rhoda would inform Arthur bluntly that Grace had died 'without any friends' and been buried 'in a pauper's grave'. It was an unkind description, and perhaps not quite accurate; Grace was probably buried in the grounds of the sanatorium where she died. Either way, Rhoda had little sympathy to offer.

*

Growing up on Unity Place was not always easy. Alvin Rakoff, whom Jacqueline would later marry, believes she and Arthur did have a loving relationship with their grandmother, but that their step-grandfather could be 'a tyrant. Though I think out of necessity; he had to be. He would only put a certain amount of coal on the fire, and then if one of them would distract him and the other would sneak an extra lump of coal on, he'd be very angry with them, very upset. Money was tight.' Weekly baths in front of the underfed fire, with water strictly rationed and the whole household present, remained vivid in Jacqueline's memory, as did the relief of reaching an age where she was allowed a little more privacy. Older relatives from the neighbouring houses tried to draw her into their petty conflicts, pressuring her to lie for them or provide false alibis when they slipped out for the night; she was unimpressed with this and refused, remembering it later as a factor in her growing sense of disconnection from the family.

Domestic difficulties were layered over the practical strain of wartime. During World War II Birmingham was Britain's most heavily bombed city after London, and everyone in Selly Oak lived with the constant threat of enemy attack. Air raids began during the summer of 1940 and lasted for nearly three years. They were concentrated on the city centre and on factories, but they caused significant damage and casualties in suburban areas as well.

For a while, the children were evacuated to Wales. Alvin recalls Jacqueline telling him that 'they were together, but it was awful. It didn't work. I think by then, people knew that a lot of abuse and things like that were happening [to evacuees]. She was not happy, and she and Arthur quickly went back.' Returning home to find one of their uncles had made a bomb shelter in the Unity Place garden, they gleefully conspired to raid the emergency supply of biscuits stored inside.

In the course of relentless bombing on the night of 11 December 1940 – a week before Jacqueline turned eleven and a month after a terrifying raid had razed much of nearby Coventry to the ground – a land mine dropped two streets away from Dawlish Road. Several houses were obliterated. Local schoolboy Derek Luke, who hid under the stairs of his home during the thirteen-hour ordeal, described it later as 'the most frightening night of the war'. By morning, more than 250 people had been killed across Birmingham and hundreds more seriously injured. The frequency of such events meant shrapnel was routinely found littering Selly Oak's streets in the mornings, and children made a game of collecting it on the way to school – 'bits of anti-aircraft shells or a bit of a plane if you were very lucky' – with whoever found the biggest piece being regarded as 'top of the class'.

Jacqueline enjoyed school and did well there in spite of wartime disruption and the shortage of teachers, but on turning fourteen she was made to leave and go to work. The money saved on schooling her would be used to support her younger brother's continued education. Arthur's total lack of enthusiasm for this plan carried no more weight than Jacqueline's disappointment.

Even if a free school place had been available to her (as it would have been soon afterwards under the 1944 Education Act), she might not have been allowed to take it up; the cost of a uniform was enough to deter many families from sending their daughters to school. Girls, it was still widely felt, did not really need an education.

But there was no shortage of employment opportunities for young people in Selly Oak. The area was dense with factories: metal and chemical works, Ariel motorcycles, Wright's saddles, gunmakers Westley Richards, the Boxfoldia packaging firm. Among the most sought after were jobs at Cadbury's Bournville – famously known as the 'Factory in a Garden' – and Jacqueline, making the best of things, decided to aim for one of these.

2

'I wasn't going to let any setbacks get in the way.'
– Jacqueline Hill

T HE BOURNVILLE FACTORY COMPLEX and its surrounding village were the embodiment of a Victorian dream of progress, moulded by the reforming principles of the firm's Quaker founders. Cadbury's employees would be spared the overcrowding and deprivation that characterised so much urban industry; at Bournville in the early 1900s, physical health and moral purity were matters of priority. Workrooms were light and airy, almost domestic in scale, and wherever possible tasks were completed by hand instead of machine. There were landscaped grounds with broad paths for strolling, an ornamental lily pond, swimming baths and even a cricket pavilion. Medical care was available to anyone who needed it. Segregation of male and female workers kept everyone respectable, and a bar on the employment of married women reflected George Cadbury's firm views on the disturbing societal implications of the neglected hearth.

As decades passed and Cadbury's output grew, there were changes, but the well-being of factory employees remained a priority. Mechanisation increased and the workrooms had to be enlarged. When war came, camouflage paint and netting were used to disguise the factory's key buildings from aerial view, and it seemed to work: the Birmingham blitz hardly touched Bournville. But wartime transformed the factory and the community in a number of other ways.

Sugar and milk shortages inevitably affected the product range, but the most striking changes had nothing to do with confectionery at all. In her book *Chocolate Wars*, Deborah Cadbury describes the chocolate moulding and packing departments being converted to manufacture gun doors for Spitfires, cases for aeroplane flares and gas masks. Assorted aircraft parts, jerry cans, petrol tanks and gun mounts were created in other areas of the factory. The playing fields and village green became home to vegetable beds and grazing sheep, and there was even a Bournville Home Guard.

At its peak, Cadbury's war work accounted for the employment of two thousand people. Many of them were transferred from confectionery departments and reassigned from simple conveyer-belt tasks to skilled mechanical operations. A 1945 booklet entitled *Bournville Utilities: A War Record* describes the company's pride in the spirit of adaptability and fearlessness displayed by its staff. Filling anti-aircraft rockets in Nissen huts on the canal bank was, after all, 'just the packing of a new kind of Assortment Box', albeit with added danger and secrecy. During air raids, women working the night shift would leave the safety of bomb shelters to stand outside and cheer while 'their' rockets defended the city.

Into the midst of all this went fourteen-year-old Jacqueline on Monday, 7 February 1944, having passed a standard written test and medical check-up. She began her career with a two-day initiation period based at the factory's Day Continuation School, where Bournville employees under the age of eighteen, along with young workers from other local firms such as Kalamazoo Paper and Boxfoldia, spent one day each week on compulsory study release with full pay. English, arithmetic and physical education took up their mornings, with afternoons given over to optional subjects including music and drama. As the pupils grew older, lives were conventionally mapped out:

'household arts' would creep into the schedule for girls, while boys took a course to prepare them for National Service.

Jacqueline was assigned to the Friday group of Day Continuation School pupils. Her position for the rest of the week was in Bournville's wages office, where she settled well and would stay for the next five years. During that time – thanks largely to her new school community – her interest in acting would be awakened, developed and transformed into a route of escape from the Birmingham suburbs.

The earliest record of Jacqueline performing dates to May 1946 when, aged sixteen, she was photographed alongside other DCS pupils in costume for a production of *Twelfth Night* at Bournville's 750-seat Concert Hall. The producer was Miss M. B. Newnham, a much-loved DCS teacher who taught elocution with such enthusiasm that it was 'to many a girl the most exciting lesson of the week'. No details of casting have survived, but a review in the Girls' DCS magazine *Our Link* describes the production as 'a delightful one in every way. The magnificence of the costumes transported us to the colourful Elizabethan age, and made us forget the drab effect of to-day's rationing ... Shakespeare's humour was appreciated fully by the players, who succeeded in "saying no more than was set down for them", and so were really amusing.'

Our Link documents a cheerful, horizon-expanding social side to DCS life just after the war, with enthusiastic staff leading the children in a range of extracurricular activities. There were outings to the Potteries, and to Stratford to see Paul Scofield and Claire Bloom in *Hamlet*; there were garden parties and dances at the school. Kind, attentive teachers like Miss Newnham, who had a passion for theatre and 'the rare gift of making everyone to whom she talks feel that he or she matters a great deal in the universe', modelled an approach to life unlike anything Jacqueline had been exposed to at home, and she blossomed under their influence.

During the severe winter of 1946/7, when coal shortages made it harder than ever to keep warm at home, Jacqueline's Friday class (known as 'A5r') decided to throw a party. It was probably a Christmas party, but it also happened to fall on Jacqueline's seventeenth birthday. Another teacher, Miss Baker, described it for the *Link*: 'It is not often that the Staff are able to attend any function in the school building – or out of it for that matter – of which they have not had a hand in the organisation. Nevertheless this was the case on 17th December, 1946, when A5r invited us all to a party of their making. It was such an enjoyable evening – games, excellent refreshments, a jolly, friendly atmosphere and just the right balance between the serious and amusing to make things go with a swing.

May we all live to see many more of these enterprising parties.'

The following year, when Miss Baker adapted *Pride and Prejudice* for the DCS players, she cast Jacqueline as Elizabeth Bennet. The *Birmingham Gazette* was impressed: 'The production is a joy. There are, inevitably, many minor weaknesses in tempo and management of period mannerism and costume, but these young people really get down to the job . . . Jane Austen lovers would have no quarrel to pick with Jacqueline Hill's interpretation of Elizabeth Bennet, and Vernon Pugh is a youthful but acceptable Darcy.'

Jacqueline was on the *Link*'s Magazine Committee, but drama was clearly her main interest. In the autumn of 1947 she made her debut with the Bournville Dramatic Society, the most established of the factory's amateur dramatics groups, in Pirandello's *The Doctor's Duty*. Any employee could join the BDS, providing they showed ability; its members included engineers, forewomen, senior managers and youthful clerks. A 1926 government report entitled *Drama in Adult Education* held the Society up as a shining example of its kind: 'All classes of employees take part in the work on an equal footing [. . .] an apprentice in the laboratory had a leading part in a play produced by the head of his own department; in the subsequent production the roles were reversed. The producer of a recent production was a piece-rate setter.' Rehearsals also gave men and women a chance, still somewhat rare at Bournville, to mix socially and work creatively together.

In 1947 the *Bournville Works Magazine* was optimistic about the Society's future, naming Jacqueline as one of its notable new members. 'The BDS need not fear that the war years have denuded it of players to succeed those who have trodden its boards so often while their younger colleagues were appearing on grimmer stages. Jacqueline Hill and Ralph Hill [no relation] suggest that the BDS will not lack "juvenile leads" when they have had more training and experience – she in using her voice, he in knowing what to do with his hands.'

Shortly afterwards Jacqueline took one such lead in James Bridie's play *Mr Bolfry*, which opened at the Concert Hall on Friday 18 December 1947 (the day after she turned eighteen) for a three-night run. The play, then a recent London success, is set in a Highland manse where a group of visiting youngsters inadvertently raise the Devil. Shifting from naturalism to metaphysical fantasy and back again, it satirises Scottish Calvinist beliefs and criticises the younger generation's supposed indifference to matters of moral philosophy. Jacqueline played Jean Ogilvie, a minister's niece, who despite her name and the play's setting is a Londoner – 'a typist and teapot-carrier at the Ministry of Interference' – meaning she was spared the challenge of perfecting a Scottish accent. 'This is a difficult play to get across,' reported the *Works Magazine*, 'and, with so many speeches without movement, calls for a high standard of acting. One was pleased to see that half the cast was drawn from younger acting members of the Society, and on the whole they were adequate . . . Miss Jacqueline Hill must not be afraid of over-acting, for her interpretation of the part of Jean Ogilvie was inclined to be wooden at times . . . It is heartening to see our younger players putting up such a brave show.'

A few months later Jacqueline appeared as Mrs Higgins in a two-night run of Shaw's *Pygmalion*, this time with the DCS Drama Group; she was also responsible for the make-up. Spring 1948 brought a leading role in Alfred Sutro's *The Bracelet*, first in a triple bill of one-acts presented by the cumbersomely named Bournville Youths' Club Dramatic Section. These were followed, possibly as insurance against the audience making an early escape, by a screening of the Marx Brothers' *A Day at the Races*. A brief review in the *Works Magazine* described Jacqueline as 'outstanding'.

Soon after this, having thrown herself non-stop into work, school and amateur dramatics for the better part of a year, she was rewarded with a School Leaving Scholarship of £100 to fund a course at the Birmingham School of Speech Training. The *Link* reported that she also passed a standardised LAMDA exam: 'J. Hill,

Friday, recently gained with Honours the Bronze Medal (for Acting) of the London Academy of Music & Dramatic Art with a total of 126 marks out of 150.' Reviewing the 1948 Bournville cuttings makes it poignantly clear that some of life's exciting possibilities were beginning, tentatively, to open up before Jacqueline that summer just at the point when – although she did not know it – her long-absent mother was dying in a nearby hospital. Things might have seemed all right on the surface, but family life for the Hills remained fractured by unhappy secrets.

In December she played a small part in the BDS's *Sweeney Todd*, and early in 1949 a lead for the DCS: Elizabeth Barrett Browning in Rudolf Besier's *The Barretts of Wimpole Street*. 'Jacqueline Hill, one of several younger BDS (*Ex*-DCS) members in the cast, made an admirably restrained Elizabeth Barrett, but a few more flashes of temperament and humour would have been welcome,' observed the *Works Magazine*. 'What a pity that the part of Flush was not taken by the spaniel we saw recently in *Sweeney Todd*, instead of by the toy dog, which caused unintentional mirth! Flush had more than usual insight into human emotions and was so important in the life of Elizabeth that Virginia Woolf wrote his biography.'

Flush's role in the play is significant: the final revelation of Elizabeth's triumph over her sinister, manipulative father hangs on the dog's escape from his evil plans. Jacqueline was obliged not only to fuss over her motionless co-star ('He gets so excited when there are several people in the room!') but to work it into meaningful moments of silent business. A typical stage direction reads: 'Elizabeth picks up Flush, stands with him under her arm, and looks round the room with an indescribable expression on her face.' Despite this and other failings ('The setting was a little too attractive'), the *Works Magazine* concluded by congratulating the director on 'what was, in the main, a good production'. A more generous reviewer for the *Link* praised 'the charming voice of Jacqueline Hill as Elizabeth which, coupled with the restraint and demeanour of an invalid, made a good performance'.

At around this time Jacqueline's Bournville managers supported her in beginning work experience at the Birmingham Repertory Theatre. The Rep, established in 1913, was one of the country's best-known regional theatres. Peter Brook and Paul Scofield were among those working there during the 1940s; Thelma Barlow, who arrived in the 1950s after considerable experience in repertory elsewhere, described it as 'sort of the next shelf up, because they were much more of a classical rep'. Jacqueline later remembered being allowed to 'walk on occasionally at the Rep, where I was the dogsbody who usually helped with the coffee'.

It was evident by now that her interests were pointing her away from Selly Oak towards an acting career, but at home there was no support for this idea. Her brother Arthur had been wrestling with decisions of his own about the future; he had recently left, aged sixteen, to join the army. He and Jacqueline would not see each other again for many years. While there was no real falling out between them, the losses and upheaval of their childhood had had lasting effects, leaving them isolated from one another. 'They had nothing at home to keep them together,' explains Marjorie Hill, Jacqueline's sister-in-law. 'They didn't have an anchor at home, and they both had to make their own way . . . I think they both wanted to forget.'

Older relatives were openly disapproving of Jacqueline's ambition. They pointed to the tale of her mother's supposedly roadshow-related downfall as proof that an acting career was the swift route to moral decline. 'They were very ordinary people, and they thought that to go off acting – especially with a mother who also went off – well, it meant you were "that sort of girl", and "we don't want to know you". And "how did *you* manage to get on the stage?"'

Money was also an issue. Young actors joining repertory companies were often asked to put down a deposit, as well as providing their own costumes. For many, this was a serious obstacle. As for drama school, fees were steep and scholarships, in a time of austerity, still uncommon. Despite this, Jacqueline persisted. 'I had set my heart on acting as a career, and I wasn't going to let any setbacks get in the way of fulfilling those ambitions.'

For four weeks during the late spring of 1949, Birmingham's historic Bingley Hall was the venue for the British Theatre Exhibition, a sprawling affair organised by the Rep in conjunction with the *Birmingham Post*. Theatre, opera and ballet companies from around Britain contributed elaborate stands full of historical, technical and decorative material; there were marionette displays, a gallery full of paintings and a specially constructed theatre in which Elizabethan scenes were performed. A Baird portable television receiver, 'the first of its kind in the world', was on display. Appearances by celebrities including Dame Sybil Thorndike, Hermione Gingold and T. S. Eliot helped to bring the public pouring through the doors, with many visitors returning several times in order to ensure they missed nothing.

Jacqueline was working at this exhibition, probably in connection with her job at the Rep, when as she later told an interviewer, 'My first real opportunity came by chance . . . I saw a notice about scholarships to RADA.' The notice invited applications for the King George VI and Queen Elizabeth Coronation Scholarships, to be granted to one male and one female candidate respectively. Each award was for a fully funded two-year place at the Royal Academy of Dramatic Art and they would be given on merit only, with no consideration of financial need.

It was a rare chance, and Jacqueline made up her mind to apply. That summer, with the good wishes of her Bournville and Rep colleagues compensating for her family's lack of interest, she travelled to London for the initial audition. The field was wide open; there was nothing to stop the women's award going to someone who was perfectly able to pay.

RADA principal Sir Kenneth Barnes described a typical audition of the period in his 1958 memoirs. 'We sat at small tables set across one end of a lecture room, facing the candidate, who appeared about twelve yards away, lit by two arc lamps . . . As the candidates entered, we gauged their degree of nervousness; then what kind of coaching – if any – they had had; the quality of voice tone, the sense of spontaneity, facial expression, bodily and intellectual reactions, and deportment. Some were too nervously self-conscious to think what they were doing, or to give meaning to their speeches, others sought to show their enterprise by tearing a passion to tatters! The few, blessed with something that presaged originality and talent, and eyes that predicted a sure future, were welcomed with high marks.'

Actor and educator Hilary Wood, herself a Queen Elizabeth Coronation Scholar during the 1950s, remembers suitable candidates being called back later for a second audition before one was chosen as the winner. In 1949, the winning girl was nineteen-year-old Jacqueline.

That September, the *Works Magazine* ran an announcement accompanied by a strikingly solemn and lovely studio photograph: 'Successful: Miss Jacqueline Hill (Wages) has won a Queen Elizabeth Coronation Scholarship for two years at the Royal Academy of Dramatic Art.' Her factory employee card recorded Jacqueline's final day of work as 30 September, with an additional note: 'To take up Coronation Scholarship to RADA. Very Good. Re-employ'.

Nine days later, Sarah Brown died at home of a heart attack. Soon after her grandmother's funeral, Jacqueline left Unity Place and her dwindling network of disapproving relatives behind for good. Had she ever wanted to return, the Bournville community would certainly have welcomed her back; but she had a bigger and much brighter future in mind.

3

'She had truth on her side.'

– Jennifer Phipps

THE *DAILY MAIL* DESCRIBED RADA in 1949 as 'no different from any other university school . . . There is no glamour about the stone stairs, bare classrooms, and crowded, clattering canteen. The two-year course at RADA is hard going, and one in five fail in the first year. It is a grinding programme of voice-production, breathing control, diction, movement, mime, and, finally, acting . . . Of the women, half never find stage jobs. Men fare little better.'

'I could not have gone had not the Birmingham Corporation given me a maintenance grant,' Jacqueline later told the *Birmingham Mail*. 'In my spare time I worked as a waitress to help things out.' Sheila Hancock – another early beneficiary of the local authority grants that would come to support a new wave of British actors during the 1950s – was a year behind her on the course, and remembers being aware of Jacqueline as 'a glamorous figure in the distance':

> She was what we called 'finals' when I went. She was kind of one of the stars, you know, that one didn't speak to because she was very beautiful and very special – but I didn't know her at that time. She was an extraordinary beauty.
>
> I was very young, fifteen or sixteen. I hated it, I hated everything about RADA. It was all kind of posh girls – the boys actually were different, because there were a lot of ex-servicemen. They'd got grants if they'd been in the services during the war. They were considerably older than us, but very glamorous. It was an overwhelming experience because everybody was very sophisticated and hardly any were working class. Anybody that was, the only ones that were not rich, were people on scholarships.
>
> And scholarships were rare in those days, you know. Grants and scholarships for actors were a very rare thing. That was the only way that people without money could get in there. The majority of people were the Honourable This, and Lady That, and it was kind of like a rather good finishing school.

Sir Kenneth Barnes, then principal of what he reportedly insisted on calling 'the R-A-D-A', was, according to 1953 graduate Robert Gillespie, 'a terrible old snob who came alive on the days when the Queen Mother attended'. David McCallum, one of Jacqueline's contemporaries on the course, recalled: 'Sir Kenneth would watch our productions, and then the next day all the cast would assemble in his room for a critique. But very often he would critique one class with the plays that another class performed, because he was getting somewhat senile.'

Voice training, involving the eradication of regional or working-class accents like Jacqueline's, was a significant feature of the curriculum; RADA students of the Barnes era were expected to master received pronunciation and stick to it. Paul Eddington, another fellow student at the time, described their lessons with renowned voice teacher Clifford Turner. 'He had published a book on his subject with, at the front, a quotation from the Old Testament: "And they said to him, 'Say Shibboleth' and he said 'Sibboleth', and they took him and slew him."' At this point in his career the easy-going Turner was inclined to rely on tape recordings to pad out his lectures, while his energetic assistant singled out individual students for rapid-fire practice of tongue twisters.

Actual stage experience was not easy to come by. A land mine had blown up the Academy's main Malet Street theatre some years before, and the only performance space available to students was an inadequate basement theatre. Lecturer Hugh Miller taught the essentials of acting along somewhat old-fashioned principles that tended to divide opinion: Eddington thought his approach was hopeless, while others (including, a year or two later, Peter O'Toole) credited him as one of RADA's best teachers. Meanwhile, the popularity of the course and the fragility of RADA's financial position meant that it was constantly oversubscribed, so as Gillespie explains: 'there were so many students that no-one ever played the whole of a leading part. You were very lucky to get the whole of an act in a three-act play. Once we put on *Cymbeline* and there were eight Imogens. At one point one Imogen (Ethel Schlesinger, 5ft 2in) went into a cave and another Imogen (Linda Barrett, 5ft 11in) came out.'

The Academy's archives from this period are sparse, and its only paper record of Jacqueline's time there is a cast list from a 1951 production of T. S. Eliot's *The Family Reunion*. In this, she is indeed one of eight actors sharing the roles of Violet and Agatha (Joan Collins is another).

Despite RADA's shortcomings, Jacqueline was happy there. Her close friends included actor Jennifer Phipps, who would later move to Canada and be acclaimed for her remarkable work with Ontario's Shaw Festival over many years. 'She was my greatest friend – so great, we hated each other sometimes,' Phipps remembers. 'We shared apartments. We were all searching for our destiny . . . I truly loved and admired her. She had truth on her side.'

'She loved RADA,' Alvin Rakoff says. 'I mean, you can imagine, you're working at Bournville in a factory – and then suddenly you're in London, even if without much money. Things were very tight, and Jackie worked in pubs, worked whenever she could. She thought the course was good – she only ever talked warmly about it. She had good experiences there.'

She was a strong enough student to win a part in the 1951 'Public Show' matinee, a final-year performance intended as a showcase for agents, producers and critics. Barnes described this in glowing terms as the highlight of the academic year. 'The Public Show . . . enabled the students to escape from their cramped quarters in Gower Street to the broad open spaces of a West End stage, and to act before a full-sized audience. The judges, chosen from the professional theatre, sat together with their torches and writing pads, prepared to award the prizes boldly set out in the programme . . . while a large representative audience was agog with interest, hoping to spot future "stars". Every student in the second year naturally longed to be included in the Public Show.'

Robert Gillespie remembers it more cynically. In his year there were ninety people competing for forty-five

Public Show roles, only fifteen of which were really worth playing: 'The rest got variations on "Your carriage awaits, madam."' Jacqueline managed to beat the odds and was cast in an extract from George S. Kaufman and Edna Ferber's *Theatre Royal*, a 1920s comedy about an American theatrical family loosely based on the Barrymores. She had already begun to develop the facility with American accents that would become one of her particular skills, and drew on it here. Hugh Miller directed, and while Eddington, also in the cast, found the experience disappointing ('all about a very boring and self-centred theatrical dynasty camping around the stage being "temperamental"'), a *Times* review of the Public Show described it as 'just the kind of play needed, since it gives the students their head and encourages them to try their hands at a more extravagant sort of acting'.

The matinee took place at the New Theatre (now the Noël Coward Theatre) in front of judges Kay Hammond, John Clements, Leslie Henson, Harold Hobson and Barbara Couper. A review in *The Stage* noted 'that delightful scene of histrionic flamboyance and inconsequence, the first act of *Theatre Royal*. From many points of view this was the most successful item, Paul Eddington, Eileen Moore, Rosalind Abrahams, John Arm, and Jacqueline Hill being particularly worth watching.'

Eighteen months later, following a brief detour into regional rep, Jacqueline would take up her first West End role.

4

'I'd heard that Sam Wanamaker was auditioning
for *The Shrike*. I sent him a postcard, saying I was
coming to see him.'

– Jacqueline Hill

THE RENOWNED AMERICAN ACTOR Sam
Wanamaker arrived in London in 1951. For
several months from January 1952 he starred
in one of the year's most talked-about West End
productions, Clifford Odets' drama *Winter Journey*.

As a person of interest to the increasingly rabid
House Un-American Activities Committee,
Wanamaker had narrowly avoided a subpoena by

making this trip to Britain. In his absence he was blacklisted, and, judging that McCarthyism showed no signs of imminent decline in his home country, decided to remain in the UK a while longer. Meanwhile, MI5 was already monitoring his movements, and his correspondence (which was intercepted) reflects his awareness of that fact. Little wonder that the Pulitzer-Prize-winning *The Shrike*, with its themes of manipulation and entrapment, was the next project to catch his interest.

Shortly before Christmas 1952, the 'Chit Chat' section of *The Stage* reported: 'Jack Hylton and Sam Wanamaker have arranged to present José Ferrer's production of Joseph Kramm's play, *The Shrike*. Mr Wanamaker will play Jim Downs, the part created [in New York] by Mr Ferrer. *The Shrike*, which is a strong, taut drama, gains its name from the butcher bird. It is set in a public hospital and exposes the totalitarian methods adopted in an otherwise democratic and free-thinking country.'

Wanamaker's Stanislavsky-influenced philosophy of method acting prized truth above all else. In interviews, he emphasised his commitment to eradicating 'the phoney' from every element of his work. 'In my opinion, it is necessary to have your own yardstick ... Is what you are doing honest? Do human beings behave and think like this, and would specific human beings behave and think like this in the particular situation being dealt with? . . . In performance, the danger of the phoney remaining undetected is greater, because actors know there are technical methods of achieving effects. They sometimes want to use them without considering if they will distort or falsify.'

Jacqueline, meanwhile, had spent some time working in repertory theatre following her RADA graduation. A brief note in her BBC file says this was in Coventry, although no record of her time there has survived. Rep was regarded by many in the business as an invaluable training ground, but it was also blamed for forcing actors into habits that someone like Wanamaker might have regarded as undesirable. Its relentless cycle of new productions every fortnight – or in some cases, every week – meant that the kind of technical trickery rejected by method actors was almost an essential survival skill.

Weekly rep in particular offered next to no time for rehearsal, let alone space for reflection. Parts had to be gulped into the memory and regurgitated, nearly undigested, before a paying crowd a matter of days later. Casting was sometimes haphazard, props and costumes often only approximately right. A nuanced, psychological approach to performance was nearly impossible and might in any case have been a poor fit with the expectations of the typical rep audience, who were widely (perhaps unfairly) perceived as preferring 'the "unimportant" play that passes an evening – and means no more'.

More positively, actors with a background in rep were typically disciplined, quick to grasp the essentials of a role, and adept at covering one another's mistakes. All of these skills would, of course, take on a new importance in the context of early television drama.

Jacqueline believed that while regional rep had been a solid start to her career, she could reasonably hope for something more. 'You learn a lot [in rep],' she told an interviewer for *Lilliput* magazine, 'but it's too far away from the West End.' Early in 1952 she moved back to London and found a room in a Ladbroke Grove flat. *Lilliput* asked her what happened next.

> 'I started round the agencies,' she says sombrely. This is clearly the dark period which it will take her a long time to forget. 'The agents told me I hadn't enough experience, or that I was wonderful, and it was only a matter of time. In either case, nothing happened. But nothing at *all*.'

She took matters into her own hands, writing to the TV drama producers Eric Fawcett and Royston Morley to request appointments. These two brief letters, handwritten on pale blue notepaper, are the earliest items in her BBC correspondence file. It was, however, a West End break that came her way first.

'I'd heard that Sam Wanamaker was auditioning for *The Shrike*. I sent him a postcard, saying I was coming to see him at the Garrick Theatre.

'I sat at the back for hours, but he was auditioning someone every ten minutes. Then a man didn't turn up. I stepped in – and got a part! Whoever that man was, I love him with all my heart.'

The play had a cast of twenty-two but only five parts for women. Jacqueline, drawing upon her skill with American accents, won the 'small but vital' role of psychiatric nurse Miss Cardell. Constance Cummings, who had starred in *Winter Journey* during the latter part of its run, was again cast opposite Wanamaker as his dangerously manipulative wife, the predatory bird of the title.

The Shrike had its provincial premiere at the Royal, Brighton, on 19 January 1953. Its staging reflected its stark theme: *The Stage* reported that 'Howard Bay's settings leave a great deal to the imagination, which is a surprisingly pleasant change,' and praised the director's use of 'moments of motionless silence'. After the Brighton run came a week at the Royal Lyceum in Edinburgh; and finally, on Friday 13 February, the production opened in London at the Princes Theatre (now the Shaftesbury).

Whether or not anyone was superstitious about the unlucky date, with hindsight it slots neatly into the story of a box-office flop. London critics praised Wanamaker and Cummings highly, but some found the play itself so harsh and shocking, so 'painful and relentless' (*Daily Telegraph*), that it was nearly impossible to watch. The *Kensington Post* called it 'a depressing spectacle', and the *Daily Express* remarked, 'This grisly play . . . drops like acid on the nerves.' Londoners did not rush to spend their money on tickets, and by late March *The Shrike* had closed.

In spite of this, for Jacqueline much good came of her first and only West End role. Her performance attracted the attention of Wanamaker's agent, Kenneth Cleveland of MCA (Music Corporation of America) – a prominent talent agency based in a converted Piccadilly mansion that had once been the home of Lord Byron. It was an exciting development. Jacqueline signed with Cleveland shortly afterwards, and he immediately began approaching producers on her behalf.

Just as significantly, her work had made a positive impression on Wanamaker himself, whose high profile, energy and supportive attitude to fellow actors made him a valuable connection. It was alongside him that Jacqueline would make her television debut a few months later.

5

The five minutes that changed the life of Jacqueline Hill occurred between 9:10 p.m. and 9:15 p.m. If you were watching television at that time you saw her. Perhaps you were impressed. Perhaps you shook your head and wondered what happened to young actresses like Jacqueline Hill after their first tilt at TV.

– Evening Standard

As *THE SHRIKE*'s RUN was drawing to a close in March 1953, the BBC's television bookings manager, Holland Bennett, sent a letter round by hand to the stage door.

Dear Mr Wanamaker,

You may remember that I came round to see you about a fortnight ago with Mr Hugh Charles to tell you how much I appreciated your performance in *The Shrike*.

I am sorry to hear that the play is coming off on Saturday week, but wonder if you would care to make a short television appearance on the following Monday, 23rd March, in our *Shop Window* programme . . . Many stars, including Constance Cummings, Flora Robson, John McCullum, etc. have appeared in the drama 'spot' which lasts about six minutes. We usually do a little scene from any well known play with which the star is associated and very often introduce an up and coming young artist to play opposite him.

The producer, Henry Caldwell, is the man to tell you further details. It is enough for me to say that the programme has an audience of three to four million and has run successfully once a month for nearly a year.

Wanamaker phoned back the next day. He would be busy rehearsing a new play on the 23rd, but was very interested in appearing on a subsequent *Shop Window*; perhaps in May?

In the event, it was the June edition of the programme that Wanamaker agreed to do, for a fee of forty guineas. The scene he proposed was one from Clifford Odets' *Golden Boy*. The 'up and coming young artist' chosen to appear opposite him, her fee a comparatively modest twelve guineas, was Jacqueline Hill.

Holland Bennett's description of *Shop Window* had skirted around the fact that the programme's main purpose was to give a boost of exposure to promising new performers, thereby discovering the 'great and popular artists of the future'. As well as drama, its offering encompassed popular singing, music, opera and dance, all drawing upon new talent. Even the sets included work by student designers.

Established stars like Wanamaker were an important part of the concept, supporting and hopefully bringing out the best in newcomers like Jacqueline. But the business of bringing each month's programme together in time for its live broadcast from the BBC's Lime Grove Studios was complicated by the involvement of so many inexperienced contributors from such a variety of backgrounds. The sense of an interminable 'series of "discoveries" doing their party pieces' was to be avoided at all costs; instead, each item had to be carefully staged, rehearsed and technically polished in such a way that the programme flowed elegantly on the night. The cramped conditions of the programme's base in Lime Grove's long, narrow Studio G made this task all the more awkward.

Henry Caldwell, who was best known as the producer of a long-running Saturday night light entertainment programme called *Café Continental*, had devised *Shop Window* early in 1951 and then spent several months persuading BBC executives to give it a chance. In November of that year he wrote to the Controller of Television Programmes, Cecil McGivern, 'I am very anxious to have a chat with you about *Shop-Window . . .* This idea, I am convinced, is what Television badly needs at the moment – an inexpensive, novel and entertaining way of finding and proving potential material for the future.'

It was agreed that the programme would form part of the BBC's spring 1952 schedule. Caldwell pushed for the guarantee of a studio pre-rehearsal, to be held on the day prior to each transmission. Because resources at Lime Grove were so squeezed, this was not an easy request to grant – even *Café Continental* made do without such a pre-rehearsal – but he made a good case: 'Almost the entire cast will be new to Television, and far from being asked to do their own act before the cameras, they will be appearing as production artistes and will be required to understand studio conditions sufficiently to enable the show to move with some degree of efficiency . . . I am most anxious that with this new idea neither the production nor the newcomers should suffer.'

The pre-rehearsal idea was approved, and Caldwell pressed on with his preparations. Prompted perhaps by murmurings of concern from those who would be working alongside him, McGivern sent him a cautionary memo copied to a long list of colleagues.

This programme takes you into the fields of other Television programme sections. Each of these sections is aiming at certain standards, developing new techniques, and very importantly, is constantly engaged in delicate negotiations with outside bodies.

It is essential that you accept the responsibility of such a programme and keep very closely in touch with the various Section Heads and Organisers concerned. You cannot be a 'lone wolf' without upsetting officials inside and people outside – who always expect the BBC to speak with one voice.

In particular, I want you to work very closely with the A.H.D.Tel. on the drama sequences, letting him know your ideas, the stars you are trying to get, etc.

The A.H.D.Tel., in the BBC's opaque system of abbreviations, referred to Head of Television Drama Michael Barry. Barry was evidently troubled by the idea of Caldwell becoming involved in, or even compromising, his relationships with important stars. By chance, though, he and Caldwell happened to run into one another at that year's RADA matinee, which took place soon after McGivern's memo was issued. It was a genial encounter, after which Barry wrote to McGivern that Caldwell's 'enthusiasm and wish to co-operate quite won me over to a whole-hearted support of his plans and I will be glad to join in making it a success'.

And once the programme got under way, it was indeed a success. Admittedly, there were endless problems: ongoing wrangles over the budget ('insufficient'), the organisation of rehearsals ('a farce') and the profligacy of the monthly *Shop Window* hospitality gathering (a 'free-for-all' at which, outrageously, 'some people had *two teas*'). Caldwell's tendency to keep his colleagues in the Design and Supply section waiting past their deadlines for essential information and to then make unexpected demands for things like a full Viennese ballroom set, or 'the largest sheet of glass we can possibly obtain', generated a long trail of memos that practically vibrate with frustration. None of this, however, stopped *Shop Window* itself from being terrific entertainment.

Cecil McGivern, by early 1953, was full of enthusiasm for the show. To Caldwell, in April, he wrote, 'Many congratulations to you and to your team on this programme. It was excellent and really exciting – gay, fast-moving, polished and "star-studded". If you could keep up this standard, we would have a new major L.E. programme, well worth more time and money and a better placing.'

To the long-suffering Head of Design and Supply: 'While doing everything in our power to help you with your problem, we must all try hard to maintain a programme series like this. Television depends on programmes as good as Monday's effort.'

And, after the May broadcast, to Head of Light Entertainment Ronald Waldman: 'This was brilliant television Light Entertainment – and, in my opinion, the best L.E. show we have so far done in BBC Television. It had heart, warmth, charm, visual excitement. It made me feel very elated. And, for the first time, the Lime Grove switch-board was swamped with calls for a while. This, even though it does without humour and comics, is a major show in the making and we must treat it as such.'

After all this, expectations were high for the following month's *Shop Window* on Monday 15 June, in which Jacqueline would appear with Sam Wanamaker. Their scene from *Golden Boy* featured Wanamaker as New York boxer Joe Bonaparte and Jacqueline as his unhappy lover, Lorna Moon.

As if a chance to perform on television opposite one of the best-known actors in the country would not in itself have been thrilling enough, the timing meant that their potential audience included a new wave of viewers who had acquired television sets in time to watch the coronation of Queen Elizabeth just two weeks earlier. There were now more than two and a half million televisions in homes and public spaces around Britain – a figure that had more than doubled since the previous year. Many viewers enjoyed gathering in groups around a single set, and of course there was only one channel available to watch; so even a conservative guess at the number of people who might conceivably see her in

Shop Window led to a figure almost too enormous for Jacqueline to visualise. The total number of ticket sales for the entire three-month run of *The Shrike* was insignificant in comparison.

At *Shop Window*'s Sunday pre-rehearsal, things began badly when technical equipment belonging to the panel game *What's My Line?* was found to be scattered around Studio G, obstructing the *Shop Window* cameras. The delay caused by moving it set off a snowball effect of scheduling clashes between the performers' call times and the Lime Grove engineers' and technicians' working hours and breaks, snarling up the remainder of the day. As a result, Caldwell was unable either to rehearse his ballroom dancers or position his choir correctly for the following day's show. By the end of *Shop Window*'s official rehearsal hours – after which everyone had to clear out of the studio sharply in order to make way for *What's My Line?* – many items had yet to be run through.

An irate Caldwell, helped by his production assistant Roma Fairley, removed the choir to a cramped music room and everyone else to a cavernous storage space misleadingly known as Studio F. There they struggled through their remaining tasks, including 'a complicated detailed rehearsal of the Rhapsody on three upright pianos scattered among the scenery stacks while bits and pieces were constantly being whisked by and over us for the *What's My Line?* setup next door'.

Sam Wanamaker had to go home before he and Jacqueline were given a chance to run through her part. Caldwell stood in for him, but it was clear to everyone that having already worked on the scene at outside rehearsal, what Jacqueline really needed now was a chance to try it with television cameras around her. The same was true for others including singer Edmund Hockridge, finally performing 'Song of the Dawn' after a tension-filled day of keeping himself poised to do so at a moment's notice. At ten thirty, having spent thirteen exhausting hours at Lime Grove, everyone was at last allowed to leave.

Jacqueline finally had her camera rehearsal the following afternoon. Roma Fairley's 1958 memoir of her time at the BBC, *The Small Screen*, features an in-depth account of a chaotic rehearsal and broadcast that closely mirrors the memos on file from this particular day. Her book uses pseudonyms – Henry Caldwell is called 'Adam' – but otherwise reflects many details confirmed in the official archive, giving a flavour of the tension in the studio:

> It's a scene from *Golden Boy*, and Adam wants a lot of it in one large close-up of two heads. In order to get them both in the picture together, it's necessary that both noses are no more than three inches apart. Uncomfortable

even when communing with a best friend, but ten times worse acting a dramatic quarrel. A piece of the dialogue:

Joe: And now you're dead.
Lorna: I don't know what the hell you're talking about.
Joe: Yes you do.
Adam to John [cameraman]: They're far too far apart, shove them closer. Right, try it again.
Joe: And now you're dead.
Lorna: I don't know what the . . .
Adam: For heaven's sake, both of you, get some *feeling* into it!
Joe (enraged): Feeling, he wants *feeling*! How can I get feeling when I'm forced to snort down her tonsils!
Adam (also enraged): This is a very dramatic scene. I don't care how much you have to snort. I only ask you to do it so that people can hear you!

They are really finding it genuinely difficult to stand so close together. In a full-length play all this would have been fixed in outside rehearsals, but for a 'gimmick' like this . . . they have had only one outside run-through.

Jacqueline, speaking to *Lilliput* magazine later that summer, identified a different problem: 'At the first rehearsal, with the camera and the mike and everything, I couldn't remember a single line. The prompter had to read it for me.'

At some point during the hours leading up to *Shop Window*'s live 8.45 p.m. broadcast, Caldwell composed a long, furious memo to Ronald Waldman. In it he detailed the farcical events of the previous day's pre-rehearsal, and his expectations of disaster that evening. He asked, 'How can a show be put on under these circumstances?' and concluded (dramatically), 'I am not dramatising all this. These are facts. I can take no responsibility for what happens on the screen to-night.'

According to Fairley's version, and bearing in mind that she may well have embellished her memoir with a little extra colour, the broadcast did have its chaotic moments. When the drama spot came round, the combined factors of under-rehearsal and the young *Golden Boy* actress's inexperience made it a predictably bumpy ride.

It is obvious from the beginning that the girl is nervous, although she is playing up very nicely. Unfortunately she is off her marks, and therefore is spoiling Adam's camera angles. He starts yelling, 'John, she's out of position, sign her to get round!' John wisely uses his discretion and makes gentle movements with his hands. These have no effect as she is not used to taking this kind of cue, and the scene in the gallery rapidly becomes more interesting than the one in the studio.

'John, are you deaf? I said are you *deaf*? I said *sign* her to get round. *Two*, you can see what that silly bitch has done, can you edge round a bit left? For God's sake – keep steady, *keep steady*! I'm coming to you now. *On two: God!* I rehearsed this over and over and over. I *told* her this would happen. *This* won't do her any good. *God!* We can't even _____ well see her!' We still have four minutes of the scene to go. Martin Winchester [this is Fairley's name for the actor occupying Wanamaker's place in her narrative] now shows how very well he knows his trade. Realising exactly what is happening, and acting magnificently at the same time, he angles himself round so that at least Adam will get an excellent shot of *him*.

Adam pays him a compliment. 'Clever bastard!' he shouts, 'but at least he's given me a shot! *Now* look at that stupid ____! Look at what she's doing to me. *One* go up. *One go up*. As high as you can! Yes that's it, try and give me a shot over his shoulder. *Now* where is she going? John, tell the bitch, tell the stupid, silly bitch . . . Get her round, round, *round to camera right. Look at the ____!'*

. . . The scene is drawing to its close, but now she's gazing into the wrong camera. This is too much, he is pounding the bench in front of him.

'I told her, *I told her*, the stupid bitch. Look at him, you bitch, *look* at him as though you meant it, *this is a love scene*, you bitch, you silly, silly *bitch*!'

I bang him with all my might. He shudders and turns. Julia punches up camera four. I hold the clipboard up. He takes a huge breath and drops his shutters with a bang, then utterly quietly, in his own normal voice, he smiles sweetly at his viewers and says: 'And now for our finale.'

Jacqueline's fellow RADA student Roger Ostime has said of their generation's early work in television, 'We pitched our performances more by luck than judgement... At RADA from 1949 to 1951 there was no training for television at all, so you really had to use your common sense.' Fortunately for Jacqueline, common sense was something she had plenty of, and regardless of how things went behind the scenes, her *Shop Window* performance evidently struck the right note. As she later told *Lilliput*,

'Sam is such a wonderful actor he made me feel I could do anything. But of course I didn't know how good it was going to be.'

The first indication of how good it was going to be came from the technicians at Lime Grove. 'Even the ones who'd only seen me on their monitor sets came down to tell me they thought I was wonderful.'

Miss Hill went home to the flat she shares with two friends, wondering if this was going to be it, at long last.

The BBC's Audience Research Report for the programme reveals that while viewers felt some of the programme had been below *Shop Window*'s usual standard, they liked Jacqueline very much. (They also admired Edmund Hockridge's singing.) Cecil McGivern's opinion is unrecorded but Michael Barry was terrifically impressed, as were the various producers who raced to contact Jacqueline the following morning. She hardly had time to catch her breath – and to write a sweetly polite note of thanks to Henry Caldwell – before she was signed to star in her first film.

6

'On the morning after,' says Miss Hill, 'the
telephone rang at nine, and went on ringing all
day.'

– Lilliput

Among those who saw Jacqueline's brief
appearance on *Shop Window* was the director
John Harlow, whose crime thriller *The Blue
Parrot* was due to begin shooting at Nettlefold Studios
within the week. The days were counting down, and the
female lead had not yet been cast. Harlow, seeing in
Jacqueline a solution to this pressing problem,
instructed his producer Stanley Haynes to get hold of

her by telephone the following morning. On offer was the role of Sergeant Maureen Maguire, specialist in undercover work for Scotland Yard.

Harlow was not alone in his interest. At least four other film company 'watchdogs' contacted Jacqueline that morning, and Head of Television Drama Michael Barry even raised the idea of casting her alongside Sam Wanamaker in a full-length TV production of *Golden Boy*. But the pressure of *The Blue Parrot*'s schedule meant that Haynes couldn't wait long for her to decide about playing Maureen, and without much hesitation, Jacqueline accepted the role.

George Campey, the television editor of the *Evening Standard*, ran a feature in the paper describing the immediate shift in her circumstances: 'That Tuesday morning Miss Hill ate no breakfast. And she has had little time for leisurely meals since. A Rolls-Royce took her to collect her clothes for the Blue Parrot film. There have been appointments at hairdressers. And at night there has been study for her part. "I have not come down to earth yet," says Miss Hill.'

The film was a B picture rather than a main feature, but even so it was a genuinely good opportunity. There was still, in the summer of 1953, a measure of optimism within the industry about the immediate future of the British second feature. A prolonged production crisis at the turn of the decade had been weathered, and circuit bookings were up; new models of international co-production were bringing in cash from America; there were even some new stages being constructed. Few would have put money on the traditional double bill lasting another decade – in the face of falling cinema attendance, the trend was towards fewer and longer films – but nevertheless, *Kinematograph Weekly*'s December review of the year was cautiously positive. 'More, and more easily available finance has brought out of our studios a larger number of smaller budget pictures than has been known for a span of years, and the generally improved quality has made the line of demarcation between "A" and "B" even more hard to define than previously . . . The prospects are, perhaps, even a little more encouraging than they were at this time last year.'

Many actors certainly carved out decent careers in B films, and Dermot Walsh, *The Blue Parrot*'s leading man, was a well-known example. Walsh and his wife Hazel Court were known as 'the celebrity couple of the second features', with his performance in 1952's *The Frightened Man* a recent success. His presence opposite Jacqueline in her first film role was, if not exactly a guarantee of quality, at least a reassuring indication of the picture's prospects. So, in its way, was the record of production company ACT Films, a union-linked organisation enjoying a run of moderately successful efforts in the crime-thriller category.

Jacqueline set out bright and early to begin work the following Monday, with 'a stomach full of butterflies'. Much had changed in the week since her *Shop Window* triumph, but this time there was no Rolls-Royce: she made it to Walton-on-Thames via train and bus from her Swiss Cottage flat, before taking a wrong turn on foot and losing her way. Disaster was averted when journalist David Clayton and photographer E. G. Malindine, who had been sent along by *Illustrated* magazine to document her first day on the *Blue Parrot* set, spotted her on the street and pulled over to offer a lift.

On their arrival at Nettlefold, her unstarry behaviour made a good first impression.

> Whatever happens from now on (and everyone admits the girl has great talent), Jacqueline will never forget her first day's work at the studio . . . Her stage experience told her to listen hard, not only to her director, John Harlow, but to every one of the old hands in the studio who had any advice to offer. Everybody was very kind. They could have made it tougher, and no doubt they would have done if she had put on airs. But Jacqueline asked questions in all the right places. She got on well from the start with her leading man, Dermot Walsh – in fact, with everybody there.

Filming at Nettlefold during the 1950s took place mainly in two disused aircraft hangars, relics of the studio's wartime requisition. Malindine's monochrome photos show Jacqueline outside a brick-built dressing-room, with a cardigan over her dancing dress; laughing with Walsh as they run through a scene together; watching, cigarette in hand, as her name is painted onto a folding chair. In the background, cast and crew drink tea, adjust cameras and confer in groups. The impression is of a busy, convivial, stimulating environment. It looks like fun.

The Blue Parrot took four weeks to shoot. Its plot, based on a story by the veteran crime reporter and networker extraordinaire Percy Hoskins of the *Daily Express*, is simple, but it moves along briskly enough. Bob, Walsh's visiting American detective, strikes up a flirtatious rivalry with Maureen, Jacqueline's undercover policewoman, as they attempt to crack a murder case linked to the downmarket Soho nightclub of the title. John Le Mesurier is the smoothly villainous owner of the club; Ballard Berkeley is Maureen's weary but determined boss.

The nature of Maureen's work makes her a moderately interesting B heroine, and a scene in which she's revealed, to Bob's astonishment, as no mere nightclub dancer but the undercover Sergeant Maguire places her promisingly at the centre of the action. Another strong moment finds her alone on screen, peering through the keyhole of the club's empty office before breaking in to search for evidence. Unfortunately, before she can make much investigative progress she's captured and tied up by Le Mesurier, leaving the way clear for a resolution in which the energetic FBI approach to police work comes out slightly ahead of the Yard's plodding. (This angle could have been a half-hearted attempt on ACT's part to appeal to US distributors, without the expense of casting an actual American lead.) There is a noticeable contrast of style between Walsh – exuberantly mugging his way past a near-total inability to sustain an American accent – and Jacqueline, whose performance is convincingly natural with moments of genuine charm, if a little too restrained to really sell her as an emerging star.

Trade reviewers received *The Blue Parrot* with no sign of the excitement that had followed Jacqueline's television debut. *Monthly Film Bulletin* called it 'a competently made formula thriller' but concluded its brief review acerbically, 'Diane Watts brings a small part amusingly to life, which is rather more than can be said for the principals.' *Kinematograph Weekly*'s veteran reviewer Josh Billings saw more to praise: 'The red herrings are neatly handled by the competent cast, the comedy relief is apt and the dénouement suspenseful. Feminine appeal slight yet piquant. The picture is well staged and colourful night haunts, neatly interspersed with appropriate and expertly photographed nocturnal chases, effectively frame its rough stuff. Dermot Walsh displays boyish enthusiasm as Bob, Ballard Berkeley impresses as Chester, and Jacqueline Hill makes an attractive Maureen. The majority of the supporting types are no less eager and the dialogue is smooth. An "in the nick of time" climax completes the shrewdly carpentered job.'

At the time these reviews appeared in late 1953, Jacqueline's agent, Kenneth Cleveland of MCA, was attempting to find her a breakthrough television role. A few months had passed since *The Blue Parrot* wrapped, with the rumour mill reporting that everyone involved was very impressed with her based on the rushes. By now, though, the initial surge of interest caused by *Shop Window* had died down, leaving the hard fact of Jacqueline's limited experience more plainly in view. Although producers liked her, significant roles seemed to keep slipping through her fingers, and Cleveland actively discouraged her from accepting any smaller parts.

Her first audition for the young Canadian producer Alvin Rakoff came at around this time. She later told an interviewer that he turned her down before she could even read for the role: 'Jacqueline was sent for consideration as an English debutante-type of girl, but Alvin's greeting was "You don't look very English" and Jacqueline recalls "He didn't even listen to me."'

Instead Alvin cast Ann Hanslip in the production (a six-part serial entitled *A Place of Execution*). However, he and Jacqueline soon saw one another again: 'Weeks later we met at a party, and she was sufficiently annoyed with me to talk to me.' As *TV Guide* put it, they 'both agreed that the agent had made a mistake in sending her for the original audition. They have been agreeing more or less ever since.'

Meanwhile, the *Golden Boy* production Michael Barry had envisioned went ahead in early November, with Julian Amyes producing – but Sam Wanamaker turned down the leading part, preferring to hold out for a TV play that hadn't yet been commercially produced in Britain. Without his involvement to provide a publicity link with their *Shop Window* appearance, the inexperienced Jacqueline was no longer a strong candidate for the role of Lorna Moon. She auditioned, but lost out to Amyes' wife, Anne Allan, who was attempting to break back into acting after taking time out to look after her children. It was a terrible disappointment.

Cleveland's next approach was to producer Leonard Brett, who agreed to consider Jacqueline for a Sunday-night drama called *Golden Rain*. Brett made positive notes at her audition ('Would be excellent casting in American sophisticated parts. Has glamour'), but decided that she might be better used in another of his upcoming plays. After waiting patiently for that audition, Jacqueline again gave an strong reading; Brett was impressed, but ultimately decided the cast was too small and the part too significant for him to risk casting a relative unknown.

Writing at this point to yet another producer, Eric Fawcett, in the hope that Jacqueline might be right for his upcoming *Three Men on a Horse*, Cleveland said, 'She is going through rather a tough time at the moment, but I believe that she has great potential as an actress, and I know would not let you down if you thought she was physically right for the part.' Fawcett quickly replied to explain that the part in question had been cast before he received Cleveland's letter, but promised to keep Jacqueline in mind for the future.

While all this was going on, modelling work helped to make ends meet. In October Jacqueline was the face of a complicated week-long fashion competition in the *Daily Herald*, for which she posed in various outfits suited to particular situations such as job interviews and visits to the theatre. Readers were asked to choose the best outfit in each category and send in postcards explaining their reasoning, for the chance of a five-guinea prize. The 'committee' who would select the winner consisted of Jacqueline, the actor Richard Greene and the columnist Marjorie Proops.

As Christmas approached, *The Blue Parrot*'s producer Stanley Haynes cast her as the Fairy Blackstick in his three-part adaptation of Thackeray's *The Rose and the Ring* for the BBC, aimed at younger viewers. She then made a one-off appearance on a teenagers' magazine programme called *Teleclub* in early 1954, and may also have featured in an episode of the independently produced series *Fabian of the Yard* (gaps in the archive make it difficult to pin this down). But it was not until she broke her contract with MCA later that year that her acting career gathered momentum again. Sam Wanamaker dropped the agency at around the same time.

Throughout this period, Jacqueline wrote regularly to well-known television producers including Harold Clayton, Dennis Vance, Douglas Allen, Peter Potter, Tony Richardson, Andrew Osborn, Barry Learoyd, Campbell Logan, John Warrington, Alan Bromly and Gilchrist Calder, seeking work. Her approach – a standard one for actors at the time, who typically combed through the credits in the *Radio Times* to identify their targets – was to send a short letter or postcard with a simple, direct account of her previous experience, and politely request a casting appointment. Sometimes this was taken up. If not, the refusal often came couched in mildly encouraging terms, in which case Jacqueline waited for a month or two and tried again. Her natural inclination to 'do things properly' was bolstered by a suggestion from Michael Barry that dealing directly with producers was her best course of action; Alvin provided further moral support.

Eventually, the combination of this effort, some hard-won experience and a growing network of contacts began to show results. By 1955, Jacqueline was being cast by Alvin and others in leading television roles. Even after two years of obscurity, though, the story of her early break retained its novelty value: the day before she appeared in 1955's *The Legend of Pepito*, an *Evening News* preview ran with the headline, 'Success-in-5-Minutes Girl Comes Back on TV'.

7

For what can television drama ever be but a shadow, a substitute for the real theatre?
– Alison Macleod, *Daily Worker*

Two years passed between Jacqueline's television debut on *Shop Window* and her first major role in a TV drama, *The Legend of Pepito*, in June 1955.

By this point, the end of the BBC's monopoly was fast approaching: the launch of commercial television, following years of political hand-wringing, was scheduled for September. Questions about what precisely constituted 'good' television, particularly in relation to drama, were more pressing than ever. Would competition with ITV force an improvement in the overall quality of programmes, or would it undermine the BBC's cherished values by encouraging what some regarded as a distressingly populist approach?

The spring of 1955 had seen the BBC begin to use telerecordings – film recordings of programmes created by pointing a camera directly at a flat TV monitor during a broadcast – to repeat the original live transmission of some plays. This practice, made possible by a change in the terms set by the actors' union Equity, allowed for more flexible scheduling as the era of competition drew closer. A telerecording was made of *The Legend of Pepito* during its broadcast from Lime Grove studios on Sunday 5 June. The production had spent the previous few weeks rehearsing at St Mary Magdalene Community Hall in Holloway, with the actors, as usual, only getting access to the actual studio a day or two before transmission. *Pepito* was an ensemble piece, with a cast of thirteen including Sam Wanamaker (in the title role), Wolfe Morris, Roger Delgado and Margot van der Burgh. Jacqueline's contract shows that the fees for her portrayal of 'Jeannie' totalled forty-seven guineas initially, with an extra three guineas added after she stayed on post-transmission to appear in retakes.

In a scheduling pattern typical of that summer, the *Pepito* repeat was transmitted more than a month after the first broadcast and was billed in the *Radio Times* as a telerecording. Before this point, the BBC's established routine had been to repeat Sunday plays by means of a second live performance just a few nights later. The new approach of leaving a longer gap was stipulated by Equity in order to maximise the fees owed to performers, but it was well suited to the BBC's concerns of the moment, too: 'The BBC drama department was wary of the accusation of repetition and homogeneity, particularly since it was clear that ITV drama departments had no intention of scheduling repeat showings of their dramas in the same week, if at all.'

The Legend of Pepito was Jacqueline's first professional collaboration with Alvin Rakoff, with whom she now shared a flat in Holland Park. The script was by Ted Allan, a friend of the couple and, like Alvin, an expat Canadian. Allan had moved with his family to London in 1954 upon realising that his nonconformist politics had attracted the attention of the Royal Canadian Mounted Police. In fact, it had been the cancellation of a Canadian TV production of *Pepito* that prompted his decision to go: 'We were four days into rehearsals. I'd been paid, the sets were ready, everything was sailing, when boom, the American Advertising Agency, representing General Motors sponsoring the TV Drama series, said that the play "made fun of mass production". It was cancelled! Another play was quickly substituted. That was my cue to leave Canada.'

By mid-1955 Allan was a central figure in London's community of Canadian writers and producers, and was enjoying some success. Another of his plays (*The Ghost Writers*, about political witch-hunting in the film industry) had already won good reviews in the West End. When the BBC *Pepito* – 'his fourth TV present-ation in Britain in less than six months', and his second collaboration with Alvin – came around, it happened to coincide with a London stage version produced by Joan Littlewood's Theatre Workshop.

The stage and television *Pepito*s debuted during the same weekend. On the Friday (3 June), Littlewood's company – recently returned from Paris, where its revival of Ben Jonson's *Volpone* had been the toast of the Théâtre des Nations festival – opened a three-week run of the play at Theatre Workshop's modest Stratford base. Two days later came the live BBC transmission of Alvin's TV version.

Critic Alison Macleod of the communist newspaper *Daily Worker* saw both productions. She devoted her radio and television column the following week to comparing them, tackling the topical question of TV drama's relationship to the stage.

Never, until this week, have I had a chance to see in the theatre a play which has just been televised.

West End theatrical managements use television sometimes for their advertising, allowing the cameras to peep at bits of their plays. They reason that if they ever allowed the showing of a complete play their live audience would be lost.

I doubt this. If it's a good play people who have seen it on television might be more keen to see it in the flesh.

For what can television drama ever be but a shadow, a substitute for the real theatre?

A good and useful substitute certainly, for the members who (like myself) hardly ever get the chance of a theatre seat. But still a substitute, making us long for the real thing as cheap margarine makes us long for butter.

Macleod contrasted the BBC's detailed presentation of 'Mexico on a plate ... real guitars, real peasant baskets, actors made up to look more or less Mexican' with the spare, prop-free approach of the Theatre Workshop version, which 'made our imagination work ... Joan Littlewood's wonderful production gives us, as television did not, the contrast between the jerky, nervous movements of the American businessman, and the calm grace of the peasants.' She made a suitably *Daily Worker*-ish distinction between the 'fine individual performances' of the TV cast, and the stage performers acting 'altogether, as a team'. Her verdict: 'the whole meaning of the play was more clear on the stage.'

Macleod's was not the only paper to cover both productions. Writing in the *Daily Mail* on 4 June, Philip Purser had rather confusingly characterised Theatre Workshop's staging as 'an unmistakable TV version – disarmingly simple set, rhythmic production and clean, shining performances'. Two days later Peter Black, the paper's television reviewer, had shown himself much less impressed with the actual TV version, which he found tiresomely earnest: 'A little light relief would have come as a long-felt want.' Macleod then referred back to this comment by 'a Tory television critic' in her own review, citing 'roars of laughter' from Theatre Workshop's East End audience as further proof of live theatre's superiority.

It was probably a little unfair that the BBC *Pepito* (of which no recording survives) should have found itself held up as evidence of TV's limitations against the work of a director as extraordinary as Littlewood. Her combination of creative daring, radical politics and relentless discipline meant that Theatre Workshop was at that point arguably doing more than any other company to challenge the conventions of the fashionable London theatre. Buzz about its work had started to build, and a breakthrough was imminent: 1956 would see the first of numerous transfers to the West End, bringing the company tremendous acclaim even as its resources were stretched to breaking point. A Theatre

Workshop staging of *Pepito* was in itself a great thing for a writer like Ted Allan, but even the strongest contemporary television interpretation of his play would probably have suffered by comparison.

However, to acknowledge this instance of impressive theatrical power is not to let Macleod's sweeping 'margarine and butter' analogy stand. Even in 1955 – much earlier, in fact – those responsible for the development of television drama had ambitions far beyond recreating the stage on screen. There was certainly a debt owed to theatrical convention but, as Jason Jacobs has pointed out, TV producers had for many years been employing 'a range of stylistic features, some of them associated with theatre, some with film styles, and some with the narrative forms of literature, such as the serial or novelistic'. Actors like Jacqueline also had to master specific new techniques in order to meet the demands of intimacy imposed by TV cameras during live performance: 'The nearness of the television camera militates against the long-distance laziness in the theatre that might permit "forgeries of emotion", and meant the necessity for total control of the micro-gestures of performance (moving eyebrows, for example). This new acting was concentrated on the face, a distillation and concentration of the expansive, projective gestures required by the stage.'

Macleod's observations of the two *Pepito*s reflect precisely such a distinction. 'On television Harry Towb acted the part of the businessman very well with his face; but on the stage David Laing acts it with his whole body.' Her preference for the stage approach is clear. But she must have been aware that to compare the two directly, without acknowledging the different technical and practical contexts shaping them, was unhelpfully reductive. There was already a body of critical writing on this topic, and it was widely accepted that what the BBC's Cecil McGivern referred to as 'small-screen television' worked far better when a close-up technique was used. If, as McGivern and others were already doing, one took a long view – acknowledging television's unique qualities, while anticipating a future in which technology would allow it to develop in unpredictable ways – the short-sightedness of Macleod's argument became apparent.

Whatever the respective merits of the stage and screen *Pepito*s, the attention attracted by their coincidental timing was a positive thing for Jacqueline, increasing the chances that plenty of viewers would see her performance. She played Jeannie, well-meaning wife of a wealthy and opportunistic American businessman. During a trip to Mexico, Jeannie takes direct action against her husband's attempts to exploit the extra-ordinary basket-making abilities of the eponymous

Pepito. A newspaper preview on 4 June focused on Jacqueline, running the headline 'Success-In-5-Minutes Girl Comes Back on TV' beside a smiling photo of 'Jacqueline Hill, whose life was changed by five minutes at Lime Grove two years ago.' It suggested, 'Her phone may well be ringing again on Monday morning.'

Whether or not the phone rang, she did receive a telegram after the broadcast from her former colleagues in the Bournville wages office. According to the company's *Works Magazine*, they were 'watching with interest the career of their former colleague'. Their message of good wishes, reported the *Magazine* proudly, 'was quickly acknowledged' by Jacqueline – unlike the begging letter that, as Alvin recalls, also arrived around this time from one of her uncles in Selly Oak. 'Now that she was beginning to have a name, he wanted some money. I said, "Who is he?" and she said he was not an uncle she liked. And I said, you know, you don't even have to answer it. Just don't bother. So she never did answer it.'

Although she was now represented by Fraser & Dunlop of Wardour Street, Jacqueline continued to seek out work on her own behalf. Ten days before the repeat transmission of *Pepito* she took out her blue notepaper and wrote to a number of producers, including Tony Richardson and Douglas Allen.

Dear Mr Allen,

I'm writing to ask for an appointment to see you with a view to future casting. I have written before to you, but at the time you were in rehearsal and therefore suggested I should write again. Since that time I have appeared on television in the 'Legend of Pepito', playing 'Jeannie' the American girl.

I would appreciate an appointment to see you any time at your convenience.

Yours sincerely
Jacqueline Hill

Similar letters followed during August and September, with slight variations; to Barry Learoyd, the hopeful addition, 'It was produced by Alvin Rakoff. Perhaps you saw it?' Finally, on 29 September – a week after the Independent Television Authority began broadcasting to the London area – Jacqueline signed a contract for her next role in a BBC play, Stanley Mann's *A Business of His Own*.

8

'I love an emotional scene.'

– Jacqueline Hill

T HE EVENING OF THURSDAY 10 November 1955, when *A Business of His Own* was broadcast live, marked precisely seven weeks since the launch of commercial television in Britain. At this stage only the London area, jointly served by the Associated-Rediffusion and ATV franchises, had access to it; it would be several more months before the launch of Britain's first regional service. Still, the week's press had plenty to say on the topic. *The Times* ran a long piece contrasting the BBC's approach to producing TV drama with the technical innovations employed by commercial broadcasters; and in the *New Statesman* Tom Driberg interviewed Sir George Barnes, departing BBC director of television, who professed himself disappointed that 'so far, no new idea seems to have come out of ITV'.

Spurred on by the competition, the BBC was now broadcasting a different play each Sunday and Thursday. The need for a constant stream of suitable new material meant that alongside their considerable efforts to develop original drama, both the BBC and ITV drama departments were still relying heavily on scripts imported from the US and Canada. In this context Jacqueline's knack for American accents, honed since her RADA days by her relationship with Alvin and friendships with expats like Sam Wanamaker, remained a valuable skill. 'She was well suited to play American parts, because they were more naturalistic and her inclinations, her acting ability, went that way,' Alvin explains. 'She didn't do what every British actor in the country was doing at that time, which was exaggerating the American accent. Or they tried to do what Vivien Leigh did in *Gone with the Wind*, which was to do Southern, because that was easier. But Jackie could do any part of America. She trained, she learned, she listened. And she would ask directors, "What sort of American do you want?" That threw a lot of British directors, because to them, American was American, and they usually meant Southern, or Bronx, New York. Jackie was capable of doing them all.'

A Business of His Own is the tragicomic tale of Sam, a middle-aged Bronx elevator operator. It chronicles his attempt to move up in the world by opening his own tobacco stand, and the domestic difficulties that result. Screenwriter Stanley Mann had written the play for TV in his native Canada, where it was broadcast in November 1953. The following summer, Mann and his wife Florence sailed from Quebec City to London on the same boat as their close friend Ted Allan and his family; the anticipation of Allan's play *The Ghost Writers* being staged there had swept them all along on the journey to a new life. Mann later recalled, 'That's why we all went . . . When we landed it was raining. It rained for six weeks. Black rain. I walked down by Piccadilly Circus, Trafalgar Square, in the rain. I said, "I'm home. I found my home."' Before long he, like Allan, would become a regular at the casual Friday-night poker games attended by Jacqueline, Alvin and a rotating cast of other television people, many of them fellow Canadians.

The BBC saw *A Business of His Own* as an ideal vehicle for the ebullient Jewish American comic actor

Harry Green, who had arrived from Hollywood in the late 1940s and become enormously popular with British audiences. Green is now largely forgotten, but in 1954 Cecil Madden, the corporation's Assistant to the Controller of Television Programmes, described him as 'probably our biggest draw' in a memo noting Green's wish to move beyond light entertainment programming into radio drama. During the following year Green apparently extended this ambition to television drama, and in 1955 his appearance in the comic play *Potash and Perlmutter* was a highlight of the August Bank Holiday schedule. Late in September, producer Adrian Waller sent him the script of *A Business of His Own* for consideration, with the comment, 'I look forward to hearing that you find as much "heart" in this and in the part of Sam as I can with you at the helm.'

Green did manage to find the heart, and the BBC issued contracts a few days later to a cast including Green's *Potash and Perlmutter* co-star Meier Tzelniker, himself a significant figure in London's Yiddish theatre community, as well as the respected Jewish character actors Helen Misener and Victor Rietti. Jacqueline won the role of Sam's daughter Helen, and Ronan O'Casey, with whom she had worked on stage in *The Shrike* two years earlier, was cast as her feckless husband Henry.

Rehearsals for *A Business of His Own* began in late October in a church hall on Paddington Street. On

Wednesday 9 November, the cast moved into Lime Grove Studio D to prepare for transmission the following day. That week, Jacqueline sent postcards to half a dozen producers including Tony Richardson, Barry Learoyd and Harold Clayton, asking that they look out for her performance.

It was certain, given Green's wide appeal – a *Radio Times* preview referred in familiar terms to his 'endearing squashed lemon of a face and expressive hands', while the *Daily Mail* called him 'lovable' – that the play would draw a large audience. On the day of the broadcast, the *Evening Standard*'s 'Tonight on TV' column included a light-hearted mini-interview with Jacqueline, headlined 'She has to scream in American':

Jacqueline Hill appears in *A Business of His Own* on BBC TV tonight.

Screaming.

Miss Hill plays Helen Gold, young New York Jewish girl who has recently married. And Helen screams at her husband Henry.

'I not only scream at him, I beat him with my fists,' Miss Hill told me.

She grinned.

'You enjoy that?' I said.

'I love an emotional scene,' Jacqueline replied.

Miss Hill also loves to play Americans. She picked up the accent at drama school, when she shared a flat with two American girls. She has since made four TV, stage and radio appearances with American actor Sam Wanamaker. Has Miss Hill ever been to America? No.

'If I went there, they'd give me *English* parts, I guess,' she said.

But that would be okay. Jacqueline tells me she can scream in English too.

The following day, Philip Purser in the *Daily Mail* reviewed the play in the context of 'Mr Green's own special merits'. 'Harry Green's Yiddisher comedy headed the list the last time the BBC drama department revealed audience figures for individual plays. Last night's *A Business of His Own* should come even higher.' The *Jewish Chronicle* appreciated Green's performance and gave general praise to the play's fine supporting cast, while the *Daily Mirror* referred to its 'moving moments ... Harry brilliantly conveyed the little man's desperation'. Philip Hope-Wallace in *The Listener* all but ignored the play, making only a passing mention of it; but in the *Observer*, Maurice Richardson dropped a scathing one-line dismissal ('a woefully unreal, unviewable and nearly invisible drama') into a television column mainly concerned with assessing how the BBC was holding up against commercial TV. His verdict: rather well overall, with *Quatermass II* and *The Makepeace Story* singled out as better recent examples of the corporation's drama output; but, 'The whole thing is still in its infancy.'

Later that month, Jacqueline wrote to BBC bookings manager Holland Bennett to request that all TV bookings be sent to her personally rather than to her erstwhile agents Fraser & Dunlop. Her letters to producers about *A Business of His Own* had brought friendly replies, but it would be Alvin who, cementing their working partnership, cast her in her next two roles – one of which, by this point, was already lined up for the Christmas season.

9

The character of the woman Louise, so stiff and awkward and unsure, and so touching in its moment of thawing, was a beautiful piece of compassionate observation.

– Peter Black, *Daily Mail*

R EGINALD ROSE'S PLAY *Three Empty Rooms*, starring Jacqueline opposite the American actor George Margo, was broadcast on 27 December 1955.

It was one of seven plays in the BBC's line-up for the first holiday period of the commercial television era. Other highlights were Terry-Thomas in the comedy

Bird in Hand on Christmas Day; Harry Green in a Boxing Day farce entitled *Take It Away*; and, on 29 December, Peter Cushing in *Richard of Bordeaux* by Gordon Daviot (a pseudonym of the bestselling detective novelist Josephine Tey). ITV's seasonal drama offerings, fewer in number and rather less star-studded, included David Kossoff in *The Man Who Liked Christmas* and Leslie Dwyer in *Our Mr Dundas*. But despite the Corporation's best efforts, a Gallup poll taken earlier in the month suggested that viewers were showing a strong preference for ITV; David Kynaston recounts that '57 per cent told Gallup that ITV was better than BBC whereas only 16 per cent expressed a positive preference for BBC – a humiliating result for the Corporation.'

Three Empty Rooms had originally been produced for US television only a few months earlier. It told the story of self-conscious newlywed schoolteacher Louise and her equally awkward husband Jerry, moving in to a run-down New York apartment still empty of furniture. The theme of ordinary life and love hampered by crippling insecurity was, as a *Radio Times* preview acknowledged, strongly reminiscent of Paddy Chayefsky's warmly regarded 1953 TV play *Marty*, which had recently won even greater acclaim as a feature film. Raymond Williams has written of this period in American TV drama: 'The work of Paddy Chayefsky, from *Marty* in 1953, and of Reginald Rose and others in the middle and late 1950s, was the most creative contribution in all American broadcasting. In substance and in method . . . the feel for everyday ordinary life, the newly respected rhythms of the speech of work and the streets and of authentic privacy . . . this new television drama stimulated similar work elsewhere.'

Jacqueline's contract for *Three Empty Rooms* was issued on 1 December. Her rehearsal and performance fees totalled sixty-one guineas, a step up compared to her previous television roles. The contract mentions that this included payment for two three-hour sessions of filming, 'to be used as an integral part of this production only'.

Filmed inserts in television plays – whether library footage or, as in this case, pre-filmed scenes in which cast members appeared – were not themselves new but were beginning, in the mid-1950s, to be employed in new ways. Producers like Rudolph Cartier, remembered for a body of work including the *Quatermass* serials and a groundbreaking 1954 adaptation of *Nineteen Eighty-Four*, used film not just to provide quick transitional shots but as a means of prising open the tight box of conventional television drama, pulling viewers out into spaces beyond the studio and telling stories on a larger scale. During the 1950s there was a growing tension between those who, like Cartier and his frequent collaborator, writer Nigel Kneale, were keen to transcend the limitations of the small, cosy sets that characterised so many early BBC plays, and others who believed that such ambition would sacrifice the sense of close observation and intimacy that was TV drama's particular virtue. This debate was rooted in practical considerations as well as theory. Large sets were costly, and tessellating filmed inserts with studio material was not always straightforward. The end result could be jarring, especially if managed by a hand less sure than Cartier's. Or – depending on your point of view – it could be so effective as to override any distraction caused by a noticeable shift in image texture.

Assuming the contract is correct, filming work for *Three Empty Rooms* took place in the course of a single day (6 December) at the very beginning of the rehearsal period. Unfortunately there is no record of what it entailed, or how the material was eventually integrated into the live broadcast (Alvin, who was the producer, is not convinced it was ultimately used at all). Rehearsals then continued for two more weeks at one of the BBC's regular chilly, unheated hired spaces, the Old Oak Common Club. Cast member David Barry, then twelve years old and credited under his real name, Meurig Jones, remembers 'some of the actors, one of them being the very distinctive Bernard Bresslaw, gambling at a card school when they weren't rehearsing'. Following a two-day Christmas break, the production moved into Lime Grove on the afternoon of Boxing Day. Rehearsal that evening ran on until midnight.

Alvin had originally cast twelve-year-old Jenny Hecht, daughter of US screenwriter Ben Hecht, as a little girl living next door to Louise and Jerry. When the Home Secretary refused Jenny permission to appear (possibly for some reason connected to her father's controversial politics), eighteen-year-old Lynette Mills took over the part, although it was too late for her name to replace Jenny's in the *Radio Times*. The *Daily Mail* ran a series of photos of Mills struggling to master roller skates in preparation for her role, accompanied by an old quote from Hecht about 'British betrayers'.

This mild point of interest was eclipsed during the broadcast by a more striking aspect of *Three Empty Rooms*. The catalyst for dramatic change in the play is the offscreen birth of a baby: Louise and Jerry's neighbour goes into labour, and as they are drawn into helping her and her frightened children, Louise shakes off her own emotional paralysis. A number of viewers found the cries of pain representing the labour so distressing that they phoned in with complaints, asserting that 'this was not the sort of play to put on at holiday time' and that (although it was broadcast from 8.30 until 9.30 p.m.) it was unsuitable for children. According to a viewer quoted in the *Manchester Guardian*, the labouring woman 'screamed like someone from the Dark Ages. It was terrifying.'

Daily Worker critic Alison Macleod, never one to pull punches, objected strongly to this 'blood-curdling' aspect of the production, calling it 'atrocious propaganda against having a baby'. Her response was, she conceded, a personal one rooted in her own experiences, but it was linked to broader concerns about the BBC reinforcing unhelpful social attitudes to childbirth – thereby potentially harming far more people than those who felt concerned enough to actually complain. She devoted most of her television column to making the point:

> What, moreover, was the effect on women viewers? [...] Before an author thrusts the facts of life at his audience he should make sure that they really are the facts. And one of the facts about childbirth is that it hurts more than you think it's going to, since terror tenses all the muscles that ought to be relaxed.
>
> Because of all the propaganda in old wives' tales and novels, many expectant mothers are literally rigid with fear. The afternoon television programmes have done a good deal to inculcate a happier attitude; but, since most women work, their audience is numbered only in thousands, whereas millions must have heard those terrible screams.
>
> Their after-effects may make untold numbers of confinements more difficult.

In any case, Macleod felt, the play was a disappointment. 'Both main characters, though sympathetically played by George Margo and Jacqueline Hill, antagonise us by their self-pity. They fret about their "failure" in a way which says volumes about the conventional American conception of success.' Commercial television's *The Man Who Liked Christmas*, she concluded, was 'a far finer play'.

Comparing Macleod's review with mainstream press reports highlights a lack of consensus about early television's responsibility to ordinary viewers who might be upset by disturbing themes. The days of dedicated telephone helplines for those 'affected by the issues in this programme' were still a long way off. Cyril Aynsley in the *Daily Express* was brisk in his dismissal of the querulous complainers, and of the potential impact on society at large: 'This was a sensitive story, with superb acting from George Margo and Jacqueline Hill. Complaints? The BBC deserves credit for giving a big holiday audience an adult play.'

And Peter Black in the *Mail* was too impressed with the production as a whole to find any room in his column for controversy. 'The character of the woman Louise, so stiff and awkward and unsure, and so touching in its moment of thawing, was a beautiful piece of compassionate observation. The whole play, Alvin Rakoff's direction and the acting of George

Margo and Jacqueline Hill, made a distinguished drama offering.'

Three Empty Rooms marked a shift in Jacqueline's status from ensemble player to reliable female lead. Conscious that the stakes were high, she became unusually nervous before the broadcast – so nervous, in fact, that she came to see Alvin in the control room and told him, 'I can't go on.' He managed to talk her down. Afterwards, having made a success of the performance, she seemed more sure of herself in correspondence with producers. Her hopeful requests for general appointments shifted into a slightly more direct, confident register: 'I understand you are casting at the moment and I'm writing to ask if there is anything in the play I might read for.' She also signed again with an agent, Frederick Joachim. During the coming year, as well as taking on further BBC work with Alvin, she would appear for the first time in an ITV play.

10

'I always thought that she might have got a lot
further if she hadn't been with me.'

– Alvin Rakoff

J ACQUELINE FOLLOWED UP *Three Empty Rooms* with
a smaller role for Alvin on 15 April 1956 – a fortnight
after London's new television transmitter opened at
Crystal Palace, significantly increasing the potential
audience. The play was a BBC drama entitled *The Seat
of the Scornful*, adapted by Ted Allan from a detective
novel by John Dickson Carr. She played Cynthia Lee, 'a
sort of spoiled little rich girl', as Alvin recalls, adding, 'I
miscast her in that.' The wayward Cynthia, ward of a

judge, 'escapes sentence for attempted murder, through a succession of distinguished and highly placed persons committing perjury to save her skin'. *Listener* critic Philip Hope-Wallace praised the script as 'ingenious', elaborating, 'it is really about the meaning of murder and has an ironical slant . . . which lifts the piece above the usual puzzle'. Maurice Richardson in the *Observer*, though, dismissed it as 'too much of a madman's flytrap to grip'. Neither reviewer mentioned Jacqueline, but she featured in the BBC publicity stills: standing in one shot over the prostrate body of her lover (William Lucas), and in another leaning on a chessboard, flanked by Basil Sydney (as her father) and Finlay Currie.

Sydney had already had a long career on stage and in film. For him and many others of his generation, television acting was an uncomfortable hybrid representing the worst of both those worlds. Alvin remembers, 'Basil Sydney hated television. He was of his time. It was neither film nor theatre. You were rehearsing it, you had to do it live, so anything could happen; and unlike in film, you couldn't stop and say "wait a minute, let's do this better, let's do it again". He loathed it – hated the rehearsal period, hated the two days in the studio. In those days you had two days to prepare a two-hour show. So all you needed on the floor was an actor who hated doing it: "What do you mean, I have to move here? Why do I have to move here?" Well, because the camera's here . . .

'But Jacqueline was intrigued by television. She learned not to fight the cameras, to let the cameras come to her, to treat them as allies. We were desperately trying to learn what television could do and couldn't do. Everybody – directors, producers, writers, actors.'

A few months later, Jacqueline worked on an ITV adaptation of Jean-Jacques Bernard's classic stage play *Martine*. Zena Walker, who had been at RADA with her, played the title role, with Jacqueline as Jeanne and Robert Urquhart as Julien, the third point of their love triangle. Little information about this production survives save that Walker and Urquhart fell in love while making it, in what the *Daily Mail* called 'ITV's first rehearsal romance'. They were married by the end of the year.

Jacqueline and Alvin were not yet married themselves but had been living together for more than a year, at 48 Lansdowne Road in West London. 'I can remember talking with her about it,' he says, 'and we decided that she should move in. I can't remember if I said it or she said it. I remember the landlady being horrified that I'd taken this young woman into the flat without asking permission. I couldn't see the sense in having to ask. But she said, "I'll allow your young lady to keep on living here, because I rather like her."' He laughs. 'I wisely didn't say anything.'

The Lansdowne Road flat was less than half an hour's walk from BBC's Lime Grove and Riverside

Studios as well as the nearby Television Centre, then at an early stage of development. Today the street is lined with elegantly restored Victorian villas and fragrant gardens, sweeping gracefully uphill from Holland Park Avenue. To the east lies Ladbroke Grove; to the west are Clarendon Road and the Notting Dale district.

In the mid-1950s, before gentrification transformed the surrounding area, overcrowded slums were only a brick's throw from Lansdowne Road. Clarendon Road was regarded as 'absolutely on the borderline of slum and respectability', while the adjacent Portland Road was simply 'criminal class'. Rillington Place, then newly notorious as the location of John Christie's crimes, was ten minutes' walk to the north.

The rent controls that kept housing affordable were still in place but would be lifted in 1957, opening the way for manipulative practices by landlords keen to maximise their profits. Meanwhile, the West Indian community was becoming established locally and the racial tension that would eventually lead to the Notting Hill riots of August 1958 was already building. During the early 1950s, Oswald Mosley's far-right Union Movement reportedly had several local meeting places.

But as Alvin remembers it, all of this seemed miles away while he and Jacqueline were newly in love and making their first home together. They didn't have a suitable table for hosting the weekly poker games (those were often held at producer Henry Kaplan's home, or Silvio Narizzano's), but they happily welcomed visitors. 'We were surrounded by tranquillity. It was very quiet. It was amazing – people would come from the country-side and say, "My God, you're quieter here than we are."

'It was a very nice flat. It was the top floor – I can remember Julian Amyes coming to see us and saying, "Isn't this cosy?". It was a converted loft, basically – and so there was this narrow little staircase – a firetrap. I'm sure nobody would let you live like that today. But it was ideal for a young couple. We had a reasonable living room, and one of those narrow flat kitchens that one has in London, and quite a good-sized bedroom. The landlady put big cupboards in. And it had a trapdoor to the roof. So in good weather we could sneak up to the roof, between the chimneys. There wasn't that much room up there, but there was enough to spread out a blanket.

'I remember across the road from us lived the egg girl, the girl who did the "Go to work on an egg" campaign. There were a few show-business people around. There wasn't any feeling of the tensions that were in Notting Hill, of the racism. No, nothing like that. We were sort of removed from it. Just far enough.'

Jacqueline and Alvin wanted to wait until the time was right for them to marry, but both were conscious of the disapproval directed at them as an unmarried couple living together. 'Did Jackie mind? Yes, she did. The pressure was enormous. People, when they knew that we were living together, would lift their noses in the air and walk away. It's hard to describe to young people today, but it was so frowned upon, so unconventional.

'Within the industry, people were not as offended. I remember [actor Patrick Barr] saying to me, a couple of years after Jackie and I moved in together, "You are going to do right by that girl, aren't you?" He meant it well. I said something like, "It's none of your business." And the landlady, the bank – anything out of the business, and sometimes within the business: "Oh, yes, she *lives with* Alvin."'

He believes their relationship had an impact on Jacqueline's career. 'A lot of directors wouldn't use her. Not because of the moral thing, but because they didn't want to use the partner of a director. She might compare notes. Television was just beginning in those days, and people were very insecure.

'I always thought that she might have got a lot further if she hadn't been with me. I think it could have – *would* have been different. Yes, I helped, I gave her parts; but she was *so* talented. And I remember one director saying to me, "If she wasn't your wife, I'd use her." People were very insecure in our business.'

11

'I got a call from Jackie, saying "Have you thought of Sean?"'

– Alvin Rakoff

*R*EQUIEM FOR A HEAVYWEIGHT was the first Rod Serling play to be produced for UK television. Although the main character, 'Mountain' McClintock, is a professional boxer, Alvin described it in the *Radio Times* as 'more a melodrama of mood than of action'. It had recently been broadcast in America with Jack Palance in the lead, and in the spring of 1957 Alvin arranged for Palance to fly to London and play the part again for the BBC. In preparation, he assembled a strong supporting cast including Jacqueline, Warren Mitchell and George Margo. Rehearsals were set to begin on Monday 11 March at the North Kensington Community Centre – so when Palance's agent got in touch late on the previous Friday evening to announce, 'Jack ain't gonna show,' Alvin was thrown into crisis mode.

Serling, even before the *Twilight Zone* series made him truly famous two years later, was a writer of some reputation in America, and the Sunday night BBC drama slot was important because it drew the biggest audiences of the week. Both these factors meant expectations for Alvin's production were high. It was essential to replace Palance with someone who could be counted on to deliver an equally compelling perform-ance. 'I had the devil's own job finding a new leading man,' Alvin says. 'I searched . . . well, you can imagine. Some time on the Saturday, locked somewhere in – only part of Television Centre had been built at that time, we were in one little block of it – I got a call from Jackie, saying "Have you thought of Sean?"'

Jacqueline had seen Sean Connery on stage in the chorus of *South Pacific*, as well as on television in the minor parts he'd previously played for Alvin. They knew each other socially, too, mainly through his occasional attendance at Friday night poker games. There was only one caveat to her suggestion: 'She said, "Is he a heavyweight?" And I said, yeah, I think he probably is, why? And then she said: "The ladies would like it."

'I mean to me, he was just this rather innocent, nice guy who wasn't a bad poker player. Not great, but he wasn't bad. Took enough money off me, I think, in his time.'

Alvin asked his secretary to find out whether Connery was available, and she replied, 'Well, that's a good idea. Everybody likes Sean.'

'So later that day, Sean came in. And the next day I boiled it down to four. I remember thinking I knew it wasn't going to be Sean, because I was convinced another actor [Peter Arne] could do the part. But by the time Sean came and I had done some bits with him, I knew *he* could do it, and would do it, and it was going to be exciting. And so I gave the part to Sean. And the rest, as they say, is history.'

Alvin was right to take Jacqueline's opinions seriously. By now she had a sure grasp of her craft, and her understanding of television acting in particular had developed significantly since her first dizzying experience in *Shop Window*. In typically generous fashion, she also encouraged him to see star quality in one of the lowliest *Requiem* extras, a young and uncredited Michael Caine.

But on hearing that Alvin had cast Sean Connery, various other colleagues reacted with open scorn. As biographer Christopher Bray has pointed out, the young actor's physicality was well suited to the role of a boxer, but his previous television experience had been mainly in non-speaking parts. Now he was being given a leading man's quantity of lines to deliver – in an American accent, no less – and hardly anyone believed he was equal to the task. 'Rakoff was told over and over again that he had screwed up . . . Every day during rehearsals, [Michael] Barry stopped by to tell Rakoff he wanted Connery fired. "But I told him, 'Yes, I know Sean can't really act. But I've designed the production in such a way that whenever he is really called on to do something big I'll cut away from it to another piece of action.'"'

The decision was vindicated when *Requiem* went out on 31 March. The next day, Peter Black in the *Daily Mail* had nothing but praise for both Alvin (whom he called 'as surefooted as a cat') and Connery. 'This lovable bonehead, played with quiet certainty by Sean Connery, was a fine piece of creative characterisation . . . He is star material if ever I saw it.' Jacqueline was noted too for her portrayal of Grace, an employment agency worker who falls in love with the unhappy Mountain: 'The romantic interest was artfully restrained, with a fine sympathetic performance from Jacqueline Hill.'

Reviewers in the *Evening Standard* and the *Daily Mirror* were just as positive, and *The Stage* pronounced:

'The casting of Sean Connery, as a simple soul housed in a giant's body, was a master stroke . . . Jacqueline Hill gave a moving performance, all sympathy and tenderness, as the girl at the employment agency who tries to make the vanquished gladiator aware of the truth that the world does not consist entirely of prize-fighters, promoters, touts and gamblers.'

The Listener appreciated the individual performances, but found it difficult to take Rod Serling's echoing dialogue seriously:

> The people of 'Requiem for a Heavyweight' on Sunday were inclined to repeat themselves. When they made a point they would make it again, and then have another try so that we should be quite sure about it. Quite sure about it . . . We were grateful for the oddly wistful performance of Sean Connery as the man who was once almost the heavyweight champion of the world, almost the heavyweight champion.
>
> . . . It will probably be all right for 'Mountain'. He goes hopefully back towards the Tennessee he has forgotten, sparring with a peculiarly horrid little boy he meets in a train. I think, too, that he will write to the helpful manager of the labour exchange, who was clearly 'ensorcelled' from the moment she looked at him. (Jacqueline Hill acted her very nicely on Sunday.)

In closing, it suggested that Serling 'ought to go on his knees to Sean Connery'.

Should Connery, in turn, have gone on his knees to Jacqueline Hill? 'Sean Connery owes his career to Sean Connery,' is Alvin's view. 'It's because he did what he did with it that it worked. But he owes the fact that I gave him his first leading role to Jackie, that's for sure. And there is no doubt that there was tremendous reaction to *Requiem for a Heavyweight*, to Sean. The phone didn't stop ringing for his agent, for him. And the phone didn't stop ringing for me either.'

There was no equivalent boost to Jacqueline's career this time, although she was busy anyway with a serial beginning the following week, the BBC's six-part *Joyous Errand*. 'The springboard was always greater for the men, especially in those days,' Alvin says. 'And also, Jackie's contribution wasn't as surprising as Sean's. She had already proved that she could act. But here was this unknown, good-looking boy, who appeared and took the world by storm.'

12

Jacqueline Hill, who plays the feminine lead as an
American girl in 'Requiem for a Heavyweight',
will play another American type in the Saturday
night serial 'Joyous Errand'. In the Sunday night
play she is a quietly efficient clerk in a New York
Labour Exchange; in the serial she plays a
wisecracking American nurse.

– The Stage

THE SIX-PART BBC SERIAL *Joyous Errand*, produced by Peter Lambert, was adapted by Ian
Dallas from Denis B. Wylie's 1956 book, which
the *Spectator* called 'a tolerable Secret Service novel of

considerable ingenuity'. It is a quest story in which, for complicated reasons, the four principal characters must travel around England in search of an old shirt.

Ursula Howells and Peter Arne were cast in the two leading roles of thoughtful young widow Ruth and attractive lone wolf Richard. Jacqueline was Ruth's close friend Carrie, the 'wisecracking American nurse'; Michael Warre as Max, a bemused everyman figure, completed the group. In a preview piece, scriptwriter Dallas described Carrie as 'an extraordinary woman, rootless and with a gaiety that is all too readily discernible as desolation well disguised'.

This would be Jacqueline's first serial, and the role of a glamorous American with hidden depths should have played to her strengths. Even better, the final plot twist was to involve a shocking revelation about Carrie's part in the story. The prospect of six weeks' work was always a welcome one and the broadcast was to come from the BBC's newly converted Riverside Studios, which had just been officially opened by the Queen Mother. All in all, it should have been a positive experience – but reviews of Peter Lambert's production were lukewarm from the start, and matters did not improve as the final instalment approached. (Lambert was not a very experienced television producer; he had joined the BBC two years earlier from a position in regional theatre and would leave the business in 1958, disillusioned, to take up a career in computing.)

The *Listener* critic J. C. Trewin said of the first episode: '"Joyous Errand" began in so choking a mist of exposition that by the time we reached Cornwall, where presumably the fun began, I wanted only a cold compress and a few hours' peace. We are, apparently, in search of a shirt: I did not take to a young man who said "So you want me in some way to finalise this."'

Of the second: 'By now, doubtless, the people of the see-Britain-first serial, "Joyous Errand", ought to be my old friends; but I am on no better terms with them than during the exposition ... I find my grave attention cracking at such exchanges as "Do you really believe we can find a shirt after fourteen years." – "I must clear my husband's name."'

Trewin was not the only person with doubts about the quality of the script. On the Wednesday before the fourth episode was scheduled to air, the *Daily Express* reported: 'Actor Peter Arne yesterday walked out of the leading role in the BBC's Saturday night television serial "Joyous Errand". TV drama chief Michael Barry said later: "We were all disappointed over a script. Changes were made and then everyone was happy except Mr Arne."'

Kevin Stoney, who had recently made a strong impression in a BBC *Sunday Night Theatre* production of Seán O'Casey's classic play *Juno and the Paycock*, was drafted in to take over Arne's role at short notice. By means of some frantic rehearsing at Television Centre the situation was brought under control. But somewhat embarrassingly for the BBC, another performer – chef Philip Harben – publicly withdrew two days later from his role in that week's *Benny Hill Show*. Again the problem was the script, which Harben described to the *Daily Express* as 'degrading'. Then the following day, almost as if some sort of behavioural contagion were spreading through the corporation, Laurence Harvey dropped out of the music programme *Six-Five Special* 'because, he said, there was not enough time to learn the lines. He is the third man to drop out of a BBC programme this week.' All three programmes were scheduled for the same Saturday evening (27 April) and all three went out, no doubt with some white-knuckle moments of tension behind the scenes.

Mercifully under the circumstances, the later episodes of *Joyous Errand* were not widely reviewed, but after it had limped to a conclusion in mid-May the *Glasgow Herald* found room for a brief dig: 'Dramatically last week ended away at the bottom of the class with the final instalment of *Joyous Errand*, a series so painfully artificial that it is a wonder only one member of the cast deserted.'

It was a disappointing end to what had promised to be an interesting job. By now, though, Jacqueline had other things on her mind. She and Alvin were having problems; in mid-1957 they separated to think things over, with Jacqueline moving out of Lansdowne Road and into a flat at Grove End Gardens. From there she wrote to producer Gilchrist Calder in August about a role in an unnamed BBC production.

Since I last spoke to you a personal problem has arisen and there's a possibility I may not be in London during October. As I cannot give you an answer regarding the script for another two or three weeks, I expect you will want to cast it elsewhere. If you haven't done so in that time and I am still in London, I would be very happy to play the part for you.

Thank you for letting me read it and I sincerely hope we may work together in the future.

Calder replied to say he would be happy to wait before casting, so that Jacqueline would have a chance to decide whether she'd like to take the role. In the middle of September, she wrote to him again from Brighton's Royal Albion Hotel.

Many thanks for your letter. I received it just before I left London for Brighton, where I am making a film. Hence the strange letter heading!

I can now definitely tell you that I will not be able to be in your forthcoming production, as I am getting married at the beginning of October and I will be away for the rest of the month. I am disappointed about not being able to work with you and perhaps we can rectify this sometime in the near future. I do hope so.

Nothing in her press cuttings or Alvin's memories indicates what film she might have been working on. It could have been commercial or corporate work, or some other ephemeral type of material – numerous promotional films aimed at tourists were produced in Brighton during the 1950s – but it is also possible that the film was an excuse and Jacqueline simply needed some time away from London. It had been a busy year, full of uncertainty at work and at home. Now there was a wedding to arrange, and a new stage of life was beginning.

13

She is described as a girl with a Transatlantic
voice because her speech is neither Kensington
nor pseudo-Hollywood.

– Birmingham Mail

J ACQUELINE'S BBC RECORDS SHOW that she had an
early brush with colour TV late in 1957, signing a
contract for an experimental production entitled
Her Affairs in Order. This involved three weeks' worth
of work in October and November, for a fee of fifty-one
pounds. Her contract stated that the colour production
would not be included in the Corporation's regular
television programmes, and would only be broadcast at

times when its normal television service was not operating.

The BBC had been working on the development of colour television in some form since the end of World War II. In the mid-1950s it had begun trialling colour broadcasts of slides and 16mm film clips from its Alexandra Palace premises after hours, in a form that was 'compatible' (meaning that black-and-white receivers could pick them up). Few people saw these early trials, and still fewer saw them in colour, but over the next few years they would become more frequent and more ambitious; in January 1957, 'a special programme was broadcast and shown to a large audience of Members of both Houses of Parliament on six receivers installed in a room in the House of Lords'. Experimental colour programmes continued for another year or so from Studio A at Alexandra Palace, and this is likely to have been where *Her Affairs in Order* was made.

By early 1958, Jacqueline and Alvin were married. As he began to work more regularly for ITV contractors, she too naturally shifted her focus in that direction. Alvin's production of *Man in the Corner* (*Armchair Theatre*, 12 January) kicked off her year, followed by *Poet's Corner* for producer David Boisseau (ITV Television Playhouse, 30 May) and *The Curious Savage* for Henry Kaplan (ITV Play of the Week, 6 August). As with early BBC drama, archival material relating to early ITV plays is sparse to non-existent, and no recordings of these three productions have been preserved.

The *Armchair Theatre* series of plays, made by ABC, was broadcast to all ITV regions in a Sunday evening slot from 1956 until 1974. Sydney Newman, the pioneering Canadian producer who would later oversee the creation of *Doctor Who*, is credited with giving the series a radical overhaul from mid-1958, but *Man in the Corner* was before his time. In this American play by Ernest Pendrell, Jacqueline appeared as Florence Miller, wife of heart-of-gold working-class protagonist Joey (Bill Nagy). Joey's struggle to lose weight in order to pass a police recruitment physical seems to have supplied the main conflict of the piece. According to a brief review in *The Stage*, Nagy was 'excellent' and 'the rest of the cast gave creditable performances in a play which gave little scope for development of character'.

A little more information survives about *Poet's Corner* by the Welsh playwright Gadfan Morris. This Associated-Rediffusion production was a vehicle for Harry Green, with whom Jacqueline had worked in *A Business of His Own* three years earlier. The *Birmingham Daily Post* described *Poet's Corner* as 'a light-hearted piece about a young Welsh boy whose ambition is to become a poet, but who instead achieves fame in the boxing ring'. Gary Raymond played the poet-boxer, and Green his manager; Jacqueline was the only woman in the cast, but there's no record of the name or nature of her part. The really memorable thing about the job was that it turned out to be Green's final role. During the sixty-minute Saturday-evening broadcast from ITV's Wembley studio, it was evident to viewers that he was struggling with his lines. Just after it ended, he had a heart attack, collapsed and was rushed to Edgware General Hospital, where he died two hours later.

In Manchester that August, just before she appeared in John Patrick's *The Curious Savage* on ITV, Jacqueline 'broke away from rehearsal at Granada headquarters' to speak to the *Birmingham Mail* about her role in the play 'and to send her greetings to her friends in and around Birmingham'. Of her home city, she said breezily, 'I haven't seen much of it for the past nine years. I gather the place has changed quite a bit.'

The Curious Savage, written for the New York stage in 1950, is a gentle play depicting the relationships between a wealthy widow named Ethel Savage, the greedy relatives who conspire to lock her away, and the eccentric inhabitants of the sanatorium in which they place her. Not for the first time, Jacqueline was cast as an American nurse with a poignant secret and a pivotal role in the final act. Henry Kaplan's production also featured Lionel Blair, Laurence Hardy and a young

Maggie Smith, with veteran character performer Mona Washbourne in the leading role of Ethel. Reviewers were impressed: *The Stage* praised the play, production and cast, and the *Birmingham Daily Post* called it 'enchanting'.

Early in 1959 Jacqueline worked on an episode of ABC's half-hour drama series *The Flying Doctor*, playing a woman whose husband plots to kill her. It was a chance to experiment with another new accent: the series was set in Australia, but largely filmed at Elstree Studios in Borehamwood.

Not long after this, Alvin was offered work in New York with the well-known US producer David Susskind. After so many years of playing American roles, this would be Jacqueline's first opportunity to experience American life at first hand. In mid-April, the couple left Lansdowne Road behind and crossed the Atlantic on the SS *United States* to settle into a Manhattan apartment.

14

Sam Wanamaker as Ernie, with his solid, tired
face, was perfect ballast; Jacqueline Hill as the
wife, with the saner outlook and better
intelligence than her husband, almost reconciled
one to the sentimental fudge at the end.
                                          – *Birmingham Daily Post*

J ACQUELINE DID NOT WORK while she and Alvin
were in New York. She passed her time exploring
the city and, among other things, developing a
friendship with Verity Lambert, who would go on to
make her name as the first producer of *Doctor Who*
but was at this stage working as a production assistant.

The two women had met before, but after spotting one another across a crowded Manhattan street (Lambert apparently recognised Jacqueline by her distinctive hairstyle) they became better acquainted. Alvin recalls them charming the staff in upscale department stores: 'Because of their English accents, people kept thinking they must have a lot of money. They both told a story of how they went into Bergdorf Goodman because they saw a coat they rather liked – but that neither of them could afford – and all the coats came out: the mink, the sable, everything else. They were given tea and coffee, champagne and cigarettes, everything. They loved it.'

But for the most part, without a project of her own to anchor her to their new surroundings, Jacqueline felt out of place in New York. The stifling summer heat – so intense that a surge in air-conditioner usage triggered a major city blackout – only made things worse. She complained repeatedly of being unable to breathe; she and Alvin sometimes escaped the city by visiting his sister in Connecticut, but the problem continued.

Eventually she sought help from a doctor, who simply recommended that they go home. 'Repeatedly, he said it,' Alvin remembers. '"If you want your wife to get better, take her home." I loved New York, but I wasn't very successful with Mr Susskind. His staff and I didn't get along. So we decided it was time to go back.'

By late autumn 1959 they were in London again. Jacqueline soon immersed herself in a new role with many familiar elements: working with Alvin on a BBC production of a Rod Serling play, alongside Sam Wanamaker and Ted Allan.

The Velvet Alley had first been produced for American television in January 1959, some months before Alvin and Jacqueline's New York sojourn. A newspaper preview of the BBC version describes Alvin as having 'returned from the "Velvet Alley" in New York' to direct it – the title being Serling's name for the television industry itself, as experienced by American writers and producers. The play, written around the time Serling was developing ideas for his series *The Twilight Zone*, was pitched as a savage, hard-hitting account of the pressures that came with overnight success as a 1950s US TV writer. It depicted various ways in which the industry manipulated and crushed people, and its destructive effect on personal relationships.

It was an expensive production, requiring a cast of nearly 100 people to convey the impression of the busy studios 'where minutes are measured in dollars and dollars are measured in millions'. Sam Wanamaker's fee for playing the leading role of scriptwriter Ernie Pandish was more than 1,000 guineas once the various elements of rehearsal, performance and 'mechanical reproduction' were totted up. Jacqueline signed on via Essanay, her agents at the time, to play his wife Pat for something in the region of 250 guineas. The main players also included Allan, who had turned from scriptwriting to acting, as Ernie's faithful agent Max.

Rehearsals began in early November at the Rugby Club on Walmer Road, W11, and the live broadcast came from Riverside Studio 1 on the evening of Sunday 22 November. For the most part it went well – columnist Guy Taylor in *The Stage* called it 'smooth with some nice angled shots and slick camera work' – although as he noted, it ran a full twenty minutes over its allotted time. He also used his review as an opportunity to consider the real-life atmosphere of the British television industry in late 1959, specifically the world of commercial contractors.

> Two well-known producers were sitting opposite one another discussing a certain TV contractor. Producer A was just about to join the Company, Producer B had just left the same firm.
>
> **Producer A.** I'm looking forward to starting.
>
> **Producer B.** I wouldn't if I were you. There are plenty of knife-men there.
>
> **Producer A.** There are knife-men in all the ITV companies.
>
> **Producer B.** That's true. You're likely to be stabbed in the back at any of them but with this particular company it's the way they do it. I don't mind getting

Jacqueline with her brother Arthur, early 1930s.
(From the collection of Marjorie Hill)

Arthur and Jacqueline, early 1930s.
(From the collection of Marjorie Hill)

Jacqueline in 1943, aged thirteen.
She would begin working at
Bournville the following year.
(From the collection of Marjorie Hill)

6.402 Grace Jacqueline Hill						Born 17·XII·29	Came 7·II·44	Left 30·IX·49
No.	Department	Date	No.	Department	Date			
53	Initiation School Wages 0. 3mths prob. Reg. Staff 7	7·II·44 to 9·II·44 · V·44				To take up Coronation Scholarship to R.A.D.A. Very good. Re-employ.		

S. 3404. By 17/9947.

Jacqueline's employee card from the Bournville factory.
(Provided by Cadbury's Bournville archive)

In Pirandello's *The Doctor's Duty*, her first appearance with the Bournville Dramatic Society (1947).

A 1949 clipping from the *Bournville Works Magazine*.
(Provided by Cadbury's Bournville archive)

SUCCESSFUL

Miss Jacqueline Hill (Wages) has won a Queen Elizabeth Coronation Scholarship for two years at the Royal Academy of Dramatic Art. Mr. Michael Preston (Production) has gained the Associateship in Dramatic Art of the London Academy of Music and Dramatic Art

A RADA cast list from 1951; Jacqueline and her close friend Jennifer Phipps are both on it, as well as Joan Collins and Paul Eddington. (Provided by the RADA library)

Jacqueline in costume, early 1950s.

An image from the *Daily Herald* fashion competition, 1953.

Jacqueline on the set of *The Blue Parrot* (1953): with co-star Dermot Walsh, and (below) shooting a close-up.
(© E. G. Malindine for *Illustrated* magazine, July 1953)

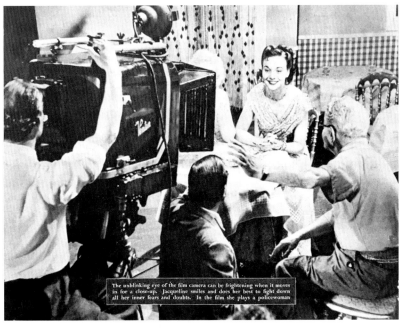

The unblinking eye of the film camera can be frightening when it moves in for a close-up. Jacqueline smiles and does her best to fight down all her inner fears and doubts. In the film she plays a policewoman

On the *Blue Parrot* set.
(© E. G. Malindine for
Illustrated magazine,
July 1953)

A snapshot of Jacqueline from the 1950s.

With George Margo in *Three Empty Rooms* (1955).

With Bill Nagy and Alvin during the making of *Man in the Corner* (1958).

With Tony Britton, probably during production of *Six Proud Walkers* (1962).

Jacqueline in the 1960s.

Jacqueline in the 1960s.

Jacqueline as schoolteacher Barbara Wright, during a camera rehearsal for *Doctor Who*'s second story, 'The Daleks' (1963).

(© Raymond Cusick)

With Carole Ann Ford (Susan) and William Russell (Ian) as the Doctor's original trio of companions in 'Marco Polo' (1964).
(© Barry Newbery)

William Hartnell as the First Doctor with Barbara and Ian, examining the remains of a Voord in 'The Keys of Marinus' (1964).
(© Raymond Cusick)

With Ray Barrett (Bennett) and Maureen O'Brien (Vicki) in the second-season *Who* story 'The Rescue' (1965).
(© Raymond Cusick)

A family snapshot, 1960s.

Jacqueline and Sasha visiting the
set of Alvin's film *Say Hello to
Yesterday* (1968).

On holiday, late 1960s.

Above and below: Jacqueline with Sasha and John.

With Patrick Ryecart and Alan Rickman during the making of
Romeo and Juliet (1978).

With Alvin and the children
during a family trip to Florida.

Jacqueline and her brother Arthur
in the 1980s.
(From the collection of Marjorie Hill)

Jacqueline as Melanie Litmayer in 'The Luncheon',
a 1983 episode of *Tales of the Unexpected*.
(ITV/Shutterstock)

Jacqueline and Alvin on the
Paradise Postponed set (1986).

During the making of *Paradise Postponed*.

stabbed in the back but it's the way they hang their hat and coat on the handle that I don't like.

The interesting thing about this story is that it is perfectly true and the contractor is one of the big four [Associated-Rediffusion, ATV, ABC-TV and Granada]. I mention it not to be cynical but to illustrate mildly how the knife-men are beginning to appear in British television. The law of the jungle is undoubtedly here but, fortunately, not as acutely as in America.

Although *The Velvet Alley* had an American setting, its pointed observations about commercial television undoubtedly resonated in Britain. By now most of the UK was receiving an ITV service and more than seven million households had multi-channel television receivers. The industry continued to grow and change swiftly, stirring up internal anxieties about power, influence and loyalty alongside the excitement of making new and challenging work. The imagery of back-stabbing, accurate or not, recurred in this context. Producer Jim Walker has recalled, 'As the 60s differed from the 50s, so Granada differed from the BBC. I was lured to Quay Street even though it meant a drop in wages . . . and even though BBC colleagues warned that GTV was infested with backstabbers.'

Phil Diack in the *Daily Herald* praised *The Velvet Alley* as 'brilliant', and the *Guardian* critic Mary Crozier appreciated the 'exuberance' of Alvin's production. Peggy Lucas in the *Daily Worker* considered it in terms of the long-term evolution of TV drama:

> No odious comparisons with the live theatre arise. Work of this kind, having taken what it needs from the parent body, has a vigorous and independent existence of its own on the little screen.
>
> ... This is a big play, made for a big budget, and presumably [the American version] made a big profit for its sponsors. It was, therefore, very interesting to watch our non-profit-making BBC loosen its pursestrings in order to accommodate this guest script.
>
> There was no sign of stint. The whole job was done with fitting big-mindedness, from top-ranking star Sam Wanamaker down to the expensive details of Hollywood settings.
>
> ... I liked it all tremendously – direction, acting and dialogue, for the important reason that it demonstrated the physical powers of tele-theatre and filled me with hope for the future.

There were some negative reviews, mainly based on disdain for Serling's script. Maurice Richardson in the *Observer* poured scorn on it. 'This was billed as showing you all the frightful things that go on behind the scenes of American television. It did nothing of the sort. We saw no Payola, no sponsors plotting to debauch the mind of the Admass, nothing but a lot of crusted corny movieland clichés about the dreadful effect of success on a playwright who broke his honest agent's heart, nauseated his plucky little wife, and his independent old Pop back in the New York tenement.'

The Listener was coolly ironic, calling the play 'another of those heartfelt American diatribes against the Bitch Goddess with a television playwright in the role of sacrificial victim' and arguing that Serling had never been likely to deliver a genuine exposé. 'With Paddy Chayefsky and Tad Mosel, Mr Serling is the third in the triumvirate of American television drama. He is held up in the *American Writers' Yearbook* as a paragon to be studied by aspirant television writers, and even in this country a Serling production counts as something of an event. Having this much in common with Ernie Pandish, his hapless hero, the author was scarcely in a position to blow the gaff on the industry.'

But there was general agreement that the performances were powerful. Reviewers praised Jacqueline, even as they acknowledged the limitations of her 'plucky little wife' role. Taylor called her 'strong in a part that has been reflected by many writers both on television and film'. US trade paper *Variety*, in its 'Foreign Television Reviews' column, said drily, 'Jacqueline Hill came over strong as the wife who could have fought off a feminine rival but not the TV industry; that's the line, believe it or not.'

Any pleasure Jacqueline might have taken in this was overshadowed by the effects of an injury she had picked up mid-performance. A BBC accident report form reveals the details:

> Nature of injury:
> *Torn ligament in back.*
> How treated:
> *X-rayed by her own Doctor and treated at Hospital.*
> How is the accident reported to have been caused?
> *Jacqueline Hill was embraced in an hysterical manner by Sam Wanamaker during the action of the Play. This was apparently aggravated by a similar occurrence at outside rehearsal.*

In fact the injury turned out to be a fracture. 'She was running towards him in elation, and he picked her up by the ribs,' says Alvin. 'She was a small, slim woman and Sam was a strong man, and in his excitement he broke one of her ribs. Of course, she carried on.'

As live broadcast crises go, it was not quite in the same league as Gareth Jones's notorious collapse and death during an *Armchair Theatre* play a year earlier (at which Jacqueline's friend Verity Lambert had been present as production assistant), nor the defibrillator burns reportedly inflicted on an *Emergency-Ward 10* actor at around the same time. Still, it was significant enough that Jacqueline had to take some time off. In

December, having made a full recovery, she wrote to the BBC's assistant booking manager Bush Bailey to reassure him: 'It wasn't anything very serious, just uncomfortable.'

It didn't put her off. With the turn of the decade approaching, Jacqueline was ready to begin one of the busiest periods of her career to date.

15

'Usually I play sad parts, but I am nothing like that in real life.'

– Jacqueline Hill

A FTER *THE VELVET ALLEY*, Jacqueline's career path diverged from Alvin's for a time. During the next few years she worked with a number of other producers on both BBC and ITV productions.

The technology of television drama continued to evolve, with more plays being pre-recorded rather than transmitted live. Patrick Dromgoole's 'ebulliently heartless' production of the classic Kaufman and Hart comedy *The Man Who Came to Dinner* (May 1960) was rehearsed in London and recorded at the BBC's Midland studio, a former cinema in Birmingham, for the Saturday Playhouse strand. Jacqueline played secretary Maggie Cutler and Leo McKern took the starring role of Sheridan Whiteside, her irascible employer. *Variety*'s foreign television reviewer approved of her –'Jacqueline Hill stood out as the long-suffering secretary whose romance threatened [Whiteside's] well-being' – but felt that 'the rest of the cast struggled gamely with an idiom that didn't come naturally'. The script had been updated and adapted for television by Gilbert Phelps, one of several writers who shortly afterwards signed on to create much-needed new drama content for ATV's *Theatre 70* slot.

The difficulty of sourcing suitable plays for television was an ongoing problem for both the BBC and commercial contractors. Standalone dramas, even more than series or serials, remained an essential element of the television schedules; the received wisdom was that they allowed space for experimentation without too much investment, making them valuable as a way of nurturing new writers and 'new, specifically televisual form, as in the celebrated collaborations of Kneale and Cartier'. This was important on one hand because there was a widespread understanding amongst those working in television that part of their job was to encourage new ideas in art and culture, and on the other because there were many hours of broadcasting time to be filled every month and a limited supply of existing plays suitable for adaptation. 'All the ages covering every great dramatist that lived could not turn out enough scripts to keep the television screens filled with plays for the allocated viewing time even for six months,' wrote critic Kenneth Baily in 1960.

Commercial television led the way in providing drama that reflected ordinary working life. Sydney Newman's reinvigorated *Armchair Theatre* strand had been doing this since early 1959; the new Granada series *Coronation Street*, when it began in December 1960, would be another prime example.

In mid-1960 the BBC drama department, conscious that it needed to keep up, subtly renamed its Sunday drama slot from *Sunday Night Theatre* to *Sunday Night Play* and devoted it to material newly written for television. Names on the initial list of contributing writers included Alun Owen, John Osborne, Elaine Morgan and N. J. Crisp. Vincent Tilsley's *The Chopping Block*, in which Jacqueline appeared as part of a relationship triangle with Ursula Howells and Glyn Houston, was the fifth play of this new strand. Vivian Matalon, who would go on to have a long and successful directing career on Broadway, produced it.

The Chopping Block was pre-recorded and has been preserved in the BBC's archive. Recording took place on

11 September in Television Centre's brand-new Studio 3, which had officially opened two months earlier. The Centre itself, an excitingly modern twelve-million-pound complex of steel and brick, was being hailed as 'the wonder and envy of television operators from every country in the world'; Studio 3, purpose-built for drama with a dead acoustic and capacity for up to six cameras, was the first of its seven studios to be completed. *The Stage* devoted a spread of several pages to this milestone. 'Dressing rooms, wardrobe accommodation, make-up, hair-styling, baths, showers, tea bars – everything is there to ensure that the performer is at his or her best before the cameras . . . Artists using the Centre will find facilities previously undreamed of. No longer will there be grumbles about the dressing rooms, about rehearsal space – or the washing facilities or rest rooms.'

The gleaming new environment was a revelation to performers long accustomed to the comparatively basic facilities at Lime Grove, Riverside or any of the commercial studios. For an actor like Jacqueline – who just over a decade earlier had been living in a cramped home with minimal plumbing and spending her days in a Victorian factory office – passing through Studio 3's enormous balanced steel swing doors represented an important step into a new era. Here was a cutting-edge space specifically designed to support performers and television staff in doing their very best work; here, there could be no question that their contribution to this forward-looking industry had real value.

The Chopping Block has a number of parallels with Ted Willis's acclaimed *Woman in a Dressing Gown*, which is best known as a 1957 film but began life as a 1956 Associated-Rediffusion play. In both dramas we see a middle-aged, working-class couple (played in *The Chopping Block* by Howells and Houston) whose marriage is failing, with the long-buried pain of losing a child making up part of their history. The husband begins an affair with a sympathetic young work colleague (played in *The Chopping Block* by Jacqueline), who tries to persuade him to leave. Eventually, realising that he is partly responsible for his wife's unhappiness, he returns home.

The similarities extend to the mirroring of structure and details. Both plays open with a domestic scene at breakfast time, where the price of cooked meats is discussed. Both homes are made uncomfortable, in different ways, by the wife's approach to household management: Amy (the eponymous *Woman in a Dressing Gown*) is hopelessly inefficient and messy, while Sarah in *The Chopping Block* channels her anger into overzealous housekeeping.

At work, both husbands share an outer office with a sympathetic, intelligent young secretary. Both secretaries offer to buy the husband a drink at a nearby pub.

Meanwhile, each wife spends time with a glamorous, extrovert friend who, it later turns out, has marital problems of her own. As we see more of the husbands' affairs, with the scene in both dramas moving to the secretary/lover's flat, the wife attempts to make herself over with a new dress (*Chopping Block*) or hairstyle (*Dressing Gown*). This effort backfires. Towards the end of each story, the husbands deliver almost identical lines to their young lovers: *Dressing Gown*'s Jim says of Amy, 'Perhaps she's what she is because I am what I am,' and *Chopping Block*'s Harry echoes, 'I'm just saying that Sarah's the way she is because I'm the way I am.' Both marriages are reprieved, but beneath the surface nobody seems truly happy.

It seems unlikely that Tilsley, a talented writer and script editor, would have knowingly tried to pass off Willis's ideas as his own, and yet once you notice the similarities it's hard to brush them aside. *The Chopping Block* may have been intended as a kind of response to the earlier play; with no paper archive surviving, it's impossible to know. Another possibility is that the parallels were unintentional. At a time when there was considerable pressure within the BBC to produce new drama that would speak to a wide audience, it is easy to imagine a busy writer unconsciously imitating a strong piece seen and admired some years earlier. In any case *The Chopping Block* does have original elements, notably a voice-over by Glyn Houston which, whenever Harry is uncomfortable or feels trapped, reveals his unspoken thoughts to the viewer. It's a clever way of illustrating the pattern he and Sarah are locked into: the sarcastic tone of his internal monologue contrasts sharply with the passivity of what he says aloud, while her exasperation increases with every inadequate reply he gives. Her efforts to spur him into action only fuel his sense of persecution and hopelessness.

The play was transmitted on 23 October. *The Times* described it as 'serious and intelligent', praising its 'taut, accurately imagined dialogue' as well as the truthful and touching performances of all three main actors. *The Listener*, however, dismissed it as pretentious and inauthentic. The implication that a 'hen-pecked husband' might in fact be responsible for his wife's unhappiness was the final straw for critic Anthony Cookman, Jr, who almost seemed to take it personally: 'Nor was I prepared, after the screeching emphasis placed on the unceasing implacability of the vixen towards her poor clerk of a mate, for Mr Tilsley's final disclosure that the entire fault for these crisis-ridden lives lay with the husband because he was wilfully and irredeemably mediocre.'

Nearly sixty years on, there is a great deal to enjoy in Matalon's production. Ursula Howells is formidable, with her furious, brittle mood in the opening scene giving way to an awkward, protective tenderness as she consoles her unhappy friend Maisie (Marion Mathie, also excellent). When Howells has screen time alone, she uses it beautifully. Houston is good too as the ineffectual, passive-aggressive Harry, whose unvoiced disdain for his wife seems progressively nastier and less defensible as the play unfolds. Jacqueline brings subtlety and intelligence to the role of senior secretary and aspiring writer Jane, a self-reliant, capable young woman whose hopes and ambitions veer just far enough away from the conventional to make happiness a little elusive.

*

After a break of a few months Jacqueline began rehearsals in January 1961 for *The Watching Cat*, a BBC 'mystery thriller' adapted by Anthony Coburn (who would later be responsible for the earliest *Doctor Who* scripts) from a novel by Pamela Fry. Set in Montreal, the play follows schoolteacher Catherine Ellis to the mansion she has inherited from an unknown, eccentric uncle. The *Guardian* described it as 'an extravagant story full of weird and sinister people; a stepmother, a drugged stepsister, and a hideously threatening cool young man in a black leather jacket'. George Foa produced, and the cast also included Ruth Dunning and Graydon Gould; recording took place at Television Centre, where Studio 4 had just opened.

Two identical cats were needed for a key scene, so the BBC approached the London Cats' Protection League for help. By chance, the League's representative had recently heard from her postman about a pair of tabby kittens abandoned in a deserted basement. After being nursed back to health, they were given the job.

> In one scene a kitten will be the apparent cause of a swerving car killing a pedestrian. In the next, switched in as fast as Foa can call 'cut to –' he will be indoors, purring contentedly. To save £200 worth of filming, both scenes will be shot 'live' in the studio.
>
> 'I needed a double for the original tabby kitten, because we could not expect him to leap from one set to the other yards away,' said Foa. 'He has misbehaved only once at rehearsals – so far – but I am not willing to trust my powers as a lion-tamer too far.'
>
> [Foa] will use black drapes, oblique lighting, and recorded street and car noises, to which actors will pre-time their movements. His 'murder car' will only appear to move.

Apart from perhaps the kittens, *The Watching Cat* was nobody's finest eighty minutes. It went out on a Bank Holiday Monday in early April and reviews were broadly negative, with *The Stage* calling the play 'boring ... it never really reached a dramatic climax and the last scenes were more of a disappointment than a conclusion'. Richard Sear in the *Mirror* tended to agree: 'When the camera tries to make the flesh creep by lingering on a simple act of ironing, there is something wrong.' The *Guardian* was gentler: 'Though the plot was rather obvious and the behaviour scarcely subtle there were some good performances and a fine air of tension.'

Jacqueline was busy enough to move quickly on, although the response to her next play was hardly more positive. Frederic Raphael's *The Executioners* was broadcast later that month in the new Sunday-evening *Drama '61* slot (ATV), which ITV was now alternating week by week with *Armchair Theatre* (ABC) in order to keep both independent contractors happy. Geoffrey Nethercott produced, and Jacqueline starred along with William Sylvester and Derek Francis. The plot centred on a wealthy Jewish couple who, while on holiday in Spain, happen to discover that the proprietor of their remote hotel is a German war criminal.

'The obvious connection was with Eichmann,' observed Stewart Lane in the *Daily Worker*; however, owing to a convoluted denouement in which the war criminal turned out to be Jewish and Sylvester's protagonist felt unable to take the revenge he craved, the play's inadvertent message was 'not anti-fascism – quite the reverse'. *The Stage* agreed, employing capitals for emphasis – 'A play that DIDN'T make its point at all well' – above a publicity image of Jacqueline. Its reviewer was equally unimpressed with performances and script, describing her as 'not very happy in her part' and Sylvester as 'contrivedly agonised'. Elsewhere, the *Birmingham Post*'s reviewer saw the play as confirmation of a trend he had previously identified with disapproval: '[W]e are getting an increasing number of plays which are not plays in the accepted sense, but dramatic essays on sensational contemporary events'.

The week in which *The Executioners* aired also saw in the second series of the BBC's *The Men from Room 13*, centred on the undercover crime-fighting work of a secret Scotland Yard 'Ghost Squad' led by one Superintendent Halcro. In a twist on the familiar 'whodunit' structure, the audience often didn't know which character was one of Halcro's agents until the climax of the story. The series, which is now lost, featured one of the earliest BBC themes by composer Ron Grainer.

Most *Room 13* plots ran over two consecutive 30-minute episodes on Saturday evenings, but the concluding story of series two – 'The Man Who Made Trouble' – was to be a three-parter, and Jacqueline signed on to appear in all three episodes as a character named Miss Angel. Only a sketchy plot synopsis survives: the Men were in this instance attempting to smash a protection racket that was threatening small restaurants in South-East London.

There had been some difficulty finding a suitable pre-recording slot at Lime Grove for earlier episodes of the series, which may have had a bearing on the decision to transmit the final five episodes live from Studio G. There was also a late change of producer for 'The Man Who Made Trouble' from Terence Dudley to the more experienced Douglas Allen, a veteran of countless serials, series and standalone plays. Allen was one of the producers to whom Jacqueline had written seeking work in the early stages of her television career, and they now found they got on well together. The following year, they would meet again on the thirteen-part BBC serial *Six Proud Walkers*.

16

'Her stock of four-letter words was unbelievable.'
– Penny Francis

THE 1962 VERSION OF *Six Proud Walkers* was a remake and amalgamation of two shorter BBC serials originally produced in 1954–5 (*Six Proud Walkers* and *The Mulberry Accelerator*). Reworked by the head of the BBC's script department, Donald Wilson, from his own original scripts, it told the suspenseful but light-hearted story of a young actress who appears on a television panel show (Lana Morris), her detective-inspector love interest (Tony Britton) and the eccentric gang of jewel thieves with whom she becomes entangled (Jacqueline, in an enjoyable departure from her usual type of role, played one of these). Derek Francis, Andrew Sachs, Terence Alexander, Kevin Stoney and Julia Lockwood were also in the cast. Ron Grainer, by this time a sought-after composer for television, contributed the music; Douglas Allen produced, but several episodes were directed by others including Dorothea Brooking and Patrick Dromgoole.

Serials and series had one clear advantage over plays: the capacity to build up viewing figures by allowing a story to unfold over time. Wilson wrote a piece in the *Radio Times* describing the particular satisfaction he found in working on a serial: 'There is a singular pleasure in constructing an ingenious, plausible, though not necessarily possible story, that has to be told in a particular sort of way if it is to hold the attention over several weeks.' He was confident that the *Six Proud Walkers* cast and production crew would function well as a team over the months that followed, and added 'I, at least, am looking forward to every minute of it.'

Douglas Allen wrote warmly to Jacqueline in late January, welcoming her to the cast. 'My dear Jackie: Both Donald and I are delighted at the thought that you are able to play the part of Senhora Romalho (Sally Walker). I don't know whether the final negotiations are completed and thought in the meantime you might like to be looking at the first four scripts.'

Jacqueline's agency contacted him soon afterwards to pin down the details, and he replied with another affectionate letter, signed 'with love'. His tone reinforces the impression given by others who worked with Jacqueline over the years that she was always well liked on set, balancing professionalism with an easy good humour. Tony Britton recalls: 'She was a tremendous woman. We had a great time with the rest of the company when we rehearsed [*Six Proud Walkers*], in one of the BBC rehearsal rooms along Fulham way. At lunchtimes we behaved badly – we all had quite a lot to drink ... I remember her as a tremendous spirit in the show, and a very good actor. Altogether a lovely woman.'

Jacqueline appeared in eight of the serial's thirteen half-hour episodes. Some filmed sequences were shot in mid-February before rehearsals got under way later that month. Recording then began on 1 March at Lime Grove Studio D; so there was a busy period of mixed rehearsing and recording that lasted until the middle of April, by which time nearly half the episodes had already aired.

More rewrites than expected were needed along the way, and Allen's production assistant left partway through the run, with the result that Allen soon found he was falling behind with planning, design and casting decisions for the second half of the serial. Fortunately the acclaimed children's drama producer Dorothea Brooking, who had already helped by directing a few of the episodes, managed to make time in her schedule for more even though she was in the midst of working on the children's serial *Katy*. 'Douglas has got into a bit of a panic [. . .] he has no-one he can really rely on,' she explained to Owen Reed, Head of Children's Programming. 'I promise I won't let Katy suffer.'

Six Proud Walkers went out on Saturday evenings at six thirty. Pre-publicity for the first episode on 10 March featured photographs of Jacqueline as 'Senhora Romalho', the diamond-stealing persona adopted by her character, Sally Walker, as part of an ingenious robbery plot masterminded by Derek Francis as 'jovial rogue' Joey. (An on-screen costume change would reveal Sally's deception to viewers near the end of the episode.) Wearing a fur coat, pillbox hat and blonde hairpiece, she smiled out from beneath the headline 'Diamond Jackie' in the *Daily Worker*. Television critics did not always pay the same attention to serials as to plays, but those who acknowledged the programme were positive; *The Stage* wrote appreciatively of Wilson's narrative skill, and summed up the opening episode as offering 'neatness, pace and a situation with distinctly intriguing possibilities'.

Allen requested authorisation for a BBC-funded cast party at the end of the run, and it may have been here that Jacqueline met Penny Francis for the first time. Penny remembers her husband, Derek, introducing them; the two women and their families would become close friends. 'Everybody took to Jackie. She was obviously beautiful – I mean, she had a *carriage*, and this huge head of hair, and she dressed outrageously. And she spoke outrageously. Her stock of four-letter words was unbelievable. There was a card game called Shit, Fuck and Damn, I remember – such fun, such fun.' Various *Six Proud Walkers* cast members including Jacqueline supplied the voices for performances staged that summer in the Francises' brick-built garden puppet theatre, which Penny credits with providing the seed for her later career as a writer, lecturer and advocate for puppetry. 'Late at night, large quantities of whisky; it was quite a starry cast. Those were the days when I didn't know much about puppetry, and I tolerated recorded voices. But they were pretty good recorded voices!'

Jacqueline's next two television appearances were on ITV, and neither programme survives in the archive. The first was an episode of the long-running Associated-Rediffusion crime series *No Hiding Place*, entitled 'The Bank Job'; it starred Raymond Francis as Detective Chief Superintendent Tom Lockhart and was produced at A-R's Wembley Studios, a former film studio in north London.

Next came an instalment of ABC's *Out of This World*, a strand of science fiction dramas mostly adapted from published short stories and introduced by Boris Karloff. The source material for Jacqueline's episode, entitled 'Medicine Show', was a 1953 novelette by the American writer Robert Moore Williams, about aliens with medicinal powers visiting Earth; her character was named Lil Harmon. Story editor Irene Shubik later remembered being amazed when, following the broadcast, letters poured in from viewers who had accepted the premise as fact and were hoping to be put in touch with the fictional healers.

At around this time – the precise date isn't quite clear, as its release was held up by problems with the distributor British Lion – Alvin was making his film *The Comedy Man*, in which Jacqueline took a supporting part. The cast was full of interesting names including Kenneth More, Angela Douglas, Billie Whitelaw, Cecil Parker, Dennis Price and Eileen Way; the script was by Peter Yeldham, adapted from a novel by Douglas Hayes. More had recently experienced a career slump after a period of tremendous popularity and the part of Chick in *The Comedy Man*, which is about the struggles of working (or not working) actors, appealed to him strongly. Although it was not a success at the box office, he would later name it as one of his favourite roles.

Jacqueline plays Sandy Lavery, whose actor husband Jack (Alan Dobie) kills himself soon after they become parents, having been compelled to give up his dreams and take a job as a night porter to support his family. This subplot gives fellow thespian Chick the opportunity to sneakily take over a piece of acting work in which his dead friend was about to be cast. Sandy appears in three scenes: one before Jack's death, and two afterwards with Chick.

Jacqueline's performance is impressively forceful, and Alvin and some of her closest friends cite *The Comedy Man* as one of the high points of her career. They are not wrong; and yet, from a distance of nearly six decades, it's hard to ignore the fact that Sandy as written lacks the complexity of many female characters in films of the same period. An unintended effect of her scenes today is to make you wish Jacqueline had had a few more opportunities to work with better material. As Tony Britton says, 'She was so bloody good – indeed, star quality. I'm very sorry that she didn't get to do more, and I'm very surprised that she didn't.'

When the film arrived on screens as a second feature in December 1964, reviews were mixed: the *Daily Mirror* praised its 'breezy comedy and touches of genuine pathos', but *The Times* summed it up as 'one of those films you would think could not go wrong except that it does'. Francis Fytton in the *Birmingham Daily Post* called More's 'the sort of performance that other actors daydream of in agents' waiting-rooms' and praised Jacqueline's 'moving and memorable' work, but he found the film itself 'fraught with clichés'.

Jacqueline's final piece of work in 1962 was an appearance in the popular BBC series *Maigret*, starring Rupert Davies as Georges Simenon's famous French detective. 'The Trap' was the penultimate instalment of the programme's third series, and was recorded in Studio 4 at Television Centre for transmission in early December. Jacqueline played Yvonne Moncin, an unsmilingly elegant woman with dark secrets. Sonia Dresdel and Aubrey Woods also appeared alongside the regular cast of Davies, Ewen Solon, Neville Jason and Victor Lucas; the director was Terence Williams.

The Rupert Davies *Maigret*s are still fondly remembered, and 'The Trap', adapted by Scottish writer Margo Bennett from Simenon's *Maigret tend un piège*, is a good showcase for their appealing qualities. Its impact is a little diminished by the poor quality of the archive copy but the atmosphere of a sticky Parisian summer is well conveyed, reinforced by all sorts of small touches in the performances and sets. Music and sound design contribute a great deal: Ron Grainer's distinctive theme draws the viewer in beautifully, and the echo of heels striking cobbles, the clinking of coffee cups and beer glasses all help to build Maigret's world.

Maigret sets a trap for a murderer by stationing undercover policewomen throughout Montmartre, with the enjoyable instruction, 'The women should wear normal summer clothes, and they must all be experts in judo.' There is a compelling sequence in which these decoy 'victims' saunter slowly through shadowy streets while everyone waits for a killer to pounce.

Jacqueline's character is married to a man accused of murder, and has an adversarial relationship with her creepy mother-in-law (Dresdel). In his 2017 book *The Changing Spaces of Television Acting*, Richard Hewett assesses her performance as offering 'firm evidence of a style of acting developed to accommodate the television studio':

In the scene where police inspector Maigret (Rupert Davies) arrives to question Marcel over a button from his suit found at the scene of the latest murder, Yvonne attempts to shield her husband from his interrogation, at times prompting or speaking for Marcel. Despite supplying her husband with an alibi, Yvonne is visibly nervous ... Hill conveys this anxiety via small but noticeable gestures, pulling incessantly at a cigarette throughout the first part of the sequence, and nervously tapping the third finger of her left hand against her right arm as Maigret asks Marcel to show him his wardrobe.

This tiny but significant gesture is an example of an actress well used to the studio set-up, aware that it is not necessary to employ overt, expansive gesticulation to signify subtext. At the end of the scene, after Marcel and Maigret have exited, Hill moves towards the camera – as opposed to the camera moving towards or zooming in on her – so that she is in close-up for a shot that conveys her character's distress. Breaking into tears, she slowly lowers her head, sobbing silently before gradually raising it again, a new expression dawning on her face that could be read either as concern for the fate of her delicate husband, or a dawning realisation of his guilt.

The gesture is choreographed to allow the camera – and so the audience – to take in a significant character beat for Yvonne, and demonstrates the experienced television actress's awareness of how to use the close-up to capture and convey a shift in mood or a mental process.

In Jacqueline's next project, *The Fixers*, a Granada Play of the Week transmitted on 8 October 1963, her skill in this type of work is again well displayed. The play was adapted by Gerald Savory from Stephen Becker's 1958 novel *Juice*, and produced by Henry Kaplan.

The setting of the play is San Francisco and the main characters in the source novel are American, so it's surprising to find on viewing *The Fixers* that Jacqueline's character, Helen Harrison, speaks with an English accent. Many others in the cast, including Lee Patterson, David Bauer, Helen Horton and Laurence Dane, are either

American or Canadian. Patterson plays Joe Harrison, a senior television executive at Pacific American Networks who knocks down and kills a pedestrian while driving home one rainy evening after too many strong drinks at the office. Although the accident is clearly Joe's fault, his well-connected boss automatically begins pulling strings to ensure that he escapes justice. Joe, rather implausibly shocked by this development, pushes back against it on principle; but even his serene and supportive wife Helen, who is pregnant with their first child, at first implores him to let the 'fixers' do their work so that he can avoid a prison term.

The Fixers feels a little heavy-handed by present-day standards – actors stride about urgently, talking about 'blowing the whole case open', and the dialogue is punctuated by emphatic trumpet stabs. But it is still enjoyable, and reviewers of the time appreciated it. Richard Sear in the *Mirror* called it 'a solid piece of drama . . . The action was crisp, the dialogue excellent, and the plot lively.' Anthea Hall in the *Newcastle Journal* liked its 'peculiarly attractive lingering quality' and 'the compelling quality of Lee Patterson and Jacqueline Hill as the top executive and his wife. The almost-authentic American-ness of it all – camera men in court, accents that came and went in moments of stress – simply added to the charm of an interesting production.'

Helen and Joe's scenes work particularly well towards the end of the play, when plot developments allow them to cheer up a little and a trace of ironic humour creeps into their dialogue. The chance to unbend slightly, to relax and be funny, serves Jacqueline well, but it was relatively rare for her to be cast in roles that allowed it. 'She was such a huge personality,' says Penny Francis. 'She used to boss us about, but with so much humour. Humour just took the edge off everything. She would have been great in some sort of comic TV series as a slightly outrageous friend next door . . . And she had that thing that very few British actors had, and that was a sort of built-in sexiness. Like Jeanne Moreau. Most British actresses just don't have it, but she had it. And I'm sorry that it wasn't exploited more than it was.'

By the time she made *The Fixers*, Jacqueline was already deeply involved with a new project for the BBC. Late in 1962 she had left her latest agent, Pat Trenfield at Essanay, and in January she had written to Angela Heathcote of the BBC's booking department: 'I'm always writing to you about a change of agent – I'm sorry about this. I think at the moment it would be better, should there be any enquiries, if you contacted me directly.' When they did so in the summer of 1963 it would be about a new series unlike anything she, or indeed anyone, had worked on before.

17

'Don't let's waste time talking about *Doctor Who*.'
— Penny Francis

THE BACKGROUND AND DEVELOPMENT of early *Doctor Who* has been studied and written about at impressive length by critics, scholars, journalists and fans; the programme's origin story has even been dramatised for television, in Mark Gatiss's *An Adventure in Space and Time* (2013). So many people contributed to its evolution, and so many threads are woven through its decades-long story, that it seems unlikely the well of *Who* analysis will ever run dry. While Jacqueline was wary of allowing her involvement with the programme to overshadow the rest of her work – and those who were close to her are at pains to emphasise that it should not define her – playing one of the Doctor's first companions was undeniably the job that secured her a lasting place in television history.

Late in 1962, producer Sydney Newman had moved from ABC to succeed Michael Barry as Head of Drama at the BBC. At that point, the drama department was already working to develop ideas for science fiction programmes that could plausibly attract a mass audience. Staff from Donald Wilson's 'Survey Group' had recently drafted a thoughtful report about 'the field of published science fiction in its relevance to BBC television drama', and followed it up with a list of possible texts for adaptation.

In the spring of 1963, a few months after Newman's arrival, it was agreed that a 52-week science fiction series should be developed to fill a slot in the Saturday evening schedule between *Grandstand* and *Juke Box Jury*. This new programme would comprise a number of shorter serials within an overarching storyline. Newman recruited Verity Lambert, who had worked for him on *Armchair Theatre* and was keen to advance from production assistant to producer, to take charge of the project; Lambert thus became the BBC's youngest producer, as well as its only female drama producer. Newman had already restructured the entire department in such a way that producers no longer had to direct – there would be a separate director and story editor for every programme, and in the case of a long series like *Doctor Who*, numerous directors would take a turn at the helm on a story-by-story basis.

It took a great deal of in-house discussion, disagreement and redrafting of format documents to reach an agreement on the programme's basic premise, but by July there were four main roles to be cast. These were science teacher Ian Chesterton and history teacher Barbara Wright, colleagues at a London comprehensive school; Susan Foreman, a teenage pupil of theirs who turns out to hail from another planet; and Susan's mysterious grandfather, known only as the Doctor, 'a frail old man lost in space and time'. Together they would be whisked through the dimensions by the Doctor's temperamental ship.

Early notes for the character of Barbara make her sound like a typical example of the roles Jacqueline often played: a schoolteacher, a figure for the audience to connect to, one of 'the ordinary people to whom extraordinary things happen'. It is easy to see why Lambert, knowing Jacqueline well, thought she would be a safe pair of hands for the part. *Doctor Who* was a dauntingly innovative project in so many ways that it needed to be anchored by rock-solid, reliable cast members who would cope with whatever the series might throw at them, and she was certainly that type of actor. The same could be said of her co-star William Russell, best known to viewers as the leading man of commercial television's mid-1950s series *The Adventures of Sir Lancelot.*

'I thought, I don't know whether Jacqueline will do this, because, you know, she was one of the quite strong actresses playing very good parts,' Lambert said in a later interview. 'And I think it just rather appealed to her, the whole idea of doing something a bit different, and she said yes, which was great.'

Jacqueline gave her only long interview about the programme to Richard Marson in 1985, for *Doctor Who Magazine.* In it, she recalls that she and Lambert saw each other at a party around the time the programme was being cast; they discussed it, and shortly afterwards Lambert got in touch to offer her the part. Her contract to play Barbara – the standard form heavily overtyped with clauses allowing for various outcomes, depending on whether the series took off – was issued on 31 July. The rest of the regular roles were filled by Russell as Ian, Carole Ann Ford as Susan, and the well-known character actor William Hartnell in the central role of the Doctor.

Meanwhile, other elements of the new programme were being pulled into place by Newman, Lambert, Wilson, Coburn, associate producer Mervyn Pinfield and story editor David Whitaker. The BBC Graphics Unit developed a title sequence, and Delia Derbyshire of the Radiophonic Workshop began the painstaking process of creating the programme's startling theme tune from Ron Grainer's minimal score.

The cast gathered for the first time at an afternoon photo call on 20 September in the Television Centre photographic studio. Carole Ann Ford initially found Jacqueline rather intimidating, but that impression soon dissipated. 'Jackie had a rather imposing personality when you first met her, for me anyway, but I think she was terrified out of her wits at first. If she was a little tense about something she would go rigid and people would think, "Oh, God, she's getting angry," but it wasn't like that, it was just that she was ice cold with fear. When I got to know her better I found she had a tendency to do this, and Jackie did say afterwards that she was slightly apprehensive about that first photo call because, like the rest of us, she didn't know how well she was going to fit in . . . We got on extremely well in the end. She was a warm, delightful, very professional lady, full of giggles and completely different to my first impression. She just wanted to make everything as much fun and as comfortable as possible for everyone, especially for new people who came into the series. Having previously worked on one or two television programs where she was made to feel somewhat out of things, she wanted to make sure this would never happen to anyone coming into *Doctor Who*.'

As Jacqueline later explained to Marson, 'In those tiny, tiny studios you had to be [quite close-knit] – we were so on top of each other that bad tempers would have been a disaster. I got on particularly well with William Russell. He shared my sort of approach to acting and liked to get on with the job with the minimum of fuss.'

Russell has often spoken about his friendship with Jacqueline. 'We had lots of shared memories because we were both Midlanders. We'd talk together in a Brummy accent.' The close relationship of their characters meant they got to know one another well during their intensive eighteen-month period of work on *Doctor Who*. 'She was really remarkable, Jackie, because she had such delicacy,' he says in a conversation recorded in 2010. 'She was a very delicate performer, in the best sense of the world. She was beautiful, and true. Always absolutely true.'

Maureen O'Brien, who played a later *Who* companion called Vicki, adds: 'Yes, she was – she never did anything too much or too little. She was very modern, in fact.'

'She was perhaps the most up-to-date of all of us,' Russell agrees.

Rehearsals for *Doctor Who* began at a Territorial Army drill hall on Uxbridge Road the morning after the photo call, with the young director Waris Hussein in charge. 'We were lucky in having people like Waris,' Jacqueline remembered. 'He was extremely sensitive, and knew how to work with actors on that kind of hectic time schedule so as to produce the best possible end result.' Less than a week later, on 27 September, the first episode, entitled 'An Unearthly Child', was recorded in Studio D at Lime Grove; but there were a number of technical problems, and when Newman watched the recording he immediately decided it needed to be done again, regardless of expense. Three weeks later, on 18 October, the re-recording took place, and this time Newman approved it. The first episode of *Doctor Who* was complete and would be transmitted on Saturday 23 November.

'An Unearthly Child' opens with schoolteachers Ian and Barbara discussing their professional concerns about Susan, a brilliant but peculiar teenage pupil. They decide it would be reasonable to follow her home at the end of the day and have a quiet word with her grandfather. When 'home' turns out to be an abandoned junkyard, they are puzzled; when they encounter the hostile grandfather, they become alarmed; and when they force their way into the police box where he appears to be keeping Susan hidden, they are overwhelmed by what they find inside. It is Barbara who leads viewers through the doors of the transdimensional ship TARDIS for the first time, darting into the police box's shadowy doorway on what she imagines is a rescue mission and then halting, shocked, as she finds herself in a stark, bright, impossibly large space. Even when you know the scene, the simplicity and ingenuity of the moment still dazzles. Whatever the viewers of 1963 expected to happen, it could not have been that.

When the episode first aired it was overshadowed by news coverage of John F. Kennedy's assassination the previous day (the cast had been in the studio when the story broke, recording the second serial). But after a repeat transmission a week later, reviewers began to show interest. Marjorie Norris in *The Stage* thought 'An Unearthly Child' 'an imaginative and intelligently written story, with four first-class actors carrying the burden of continuity'; she memorably described the Doctor as 'a pastiche of absent-minded professor, space age scientist and medieval wizard'. Her appreciation extended to the design and production, which had transported her 'through time and space more satisfactorily than I can recall ever having journeyed before – and that includes the cinema with all the trick effects at its disposal'.

It was with *Doctor Who*'s second story a few weeks later, when the adversaries known as Daleks were introduced, that the programme really began its transformation from a labour of love and professional pride into a certified pop-culture phenomenon. Barbara Wright had already been the first character to speak a scripted line in *Doctor Who* as well as the first to enter the spaceship. Now, in an episode transmitted on the Saturday just before Christmas, she became the first to encounter these iconic mutant creatures with their metal shells.

The first hint at their appearance comes in a cliff-hanger shot of Barbara edging her way anxiously through a maze of metallic corridors before turning with a gasp to see *something* with a menacingly extended plunger arm slowly approaching her. She moves slowly back until she is trapped against a wall, the tension building as she gazes at the unseen monster in horror; then she throws back her head and screams as the end credits kick in. (Barbara was not, as a rule, given to screaming, but in this situation her reaction seems perfectly justified.) That plunger arm was all viewers would see of the Daleks until the following week. Nothing about it was inherently frightening – but Jacqueline's performance, Christopher Barry's direction and Brian Hodgson's sound design combined to give it tremendous impact, as the ratings for the remainder of the serial would demonstrate.

Jacqueline's memory of meeting the Daleks was still vivid twenty years later. 'We were all absolutely fascinated with them. It became very easy to suspend one's disbelief when acting opposite one of those things, and that helped make the whole thing that little bit more polished and exciting . . . They were just so effective, even though they were such scene-stealers too. One could almost put up with the lessened part to be in one of those Dalek stories, because they were such fun to make.'

From an early stage on the first year of *Doctor Who*, the performances of the regular cast fed back into how their characters were written, contributing to the establishment of an essential Doctor/companion dynamic that would continue to resonate through future incarnations. As the various serials had different writers, the actors' work was all the more important to character development. 'All I was actually told was that my character was a very learned history teacher and that I was there to represent the Earth point of view. Everything else I had to put in myself, and this meant taking it up with either Verity or the director concerned,' Jacqueline remembered. 'They were usually very good and listened to me on those points, because I knew the character better than anybody else.'

It wasn't only a case of requesting tweaks to the script, but of delivering a fully committed performance that could transcend weaknesses in the writing. A scene in *The Edge of Destruction* – a much-maligned two-episode serial, written at speed to fill an unexpected gap in the production schedule early in season one – is a good example of this. The Doctor has wrongly accused Ian and Barbara of sabotaging the TARDIS, and Barbara is outraged; there is an angry confrontation. Robert Shearman and Toby Hadoke discuss the episode in their book *Running Through Corridors*, with Shearman observing that Jacqueline 'in spite of the odds actually mines something emotional and true out of all the weirdness'. Hadoke picks up the thread: 'You're right, though, to highlight Jacqueline Hill, who delivers a smashing retort to the Doctor's paranoia and accusations that she and Ian have sabotaged the Ship. Not for nothing has this fantastic confrontation – where Barbara, bristling with principled and righteous anger, really sticks it to the old man – been cited by some commentators as a turning point in the Doctor's character, and therefore in the entire series.'

The first season of *Doctor Who* consisted of forty-two episodes divided into eight serials. In order to maximise the programme's educational value, they alternated between historical and futuristic or alien settings. Jacqueline preferred the historical ones, 'because I was given a bit more to do in them ... I adored all the dressing up that went with doing the historical stories, and they were much more colourful for us because the historical sets were so gorgeous to act in. All that was lost on screen, of course, but it helped create a special atmosphere in the studio. The historicals tended to treat us far more as characters, so that there was really some acting to do.' *The Aztecs* and *The Crusades* were her favourites: 'In *The Aztecs* I had the most magnificent headdress, which was terribly difficult to balance, but which looked superb and made me feel very regal.' During *The Romans* she and Derek Francis, who was making a guest appearance as Emperor Nero, pleaded for a BBC photo call to showcase the loveliness of everyone's costumes, but were turned down on the grounds that it would take too much time.

Cast and crew worked on until the end of October 1964, by which point they had also completed the first two serials (or 'adventures') of season two. Carole Ann Ford would not return to the programme after those had aired. Unhappy with the limitations of her part, she had decided to move on, and the character of Susan was written out. Her final adventure, *The Dalek Invasion of Earth*, was transmitted in November and December in the midst of a pre-Christmas craze for Dalek-related merchandise including sweet cigarettes, comics, battery-operated toy Daleks and a board game. In one scene Jacqueline drove a vintage dustcart through a blockade of Daleks; in another, she and Ann Davies had to run across Westminster Bridge as if pursued while pushing actor Alan Judd in a wheelchair – a task which, according to Jacqueline, 'soon lost its novelty value'. This was one of *Doctor Who*'s first pieces of location work, and took place at dawn on a Sunday to minimise the chance of passers-by wandering into shot.

Davies, who played a character called Jenny, would eventually become one of Jacqueline's dearest friends, but they had not met before working together on this serial. 'She was terrifically kind and helpful and friendly,' Davies remembered later. 'She had been in the series from the beginning, so she knew how it all ran. I had to jump on the dustcart while it was moving and being driven by Jackie, and it was very old and very heavy for her to drive. And she said, "You do realise, I can't *absolutely* slow down, so, you know – d'you think you're going to be able to jump on?" And I said, yes, I think I will . . . I thought she was splendid.' The resulting scene, in which they sweep past the corpse of a rebel leader as Davies scrambles into the vehicle, is a minor highlight of one of the First Doctor's best-remembered stories.

Carole Ann Ford's successor in the TARDIS was Maureen O'Brien. She joined the cast when work resumed in mid-November for the second production block, which continued throughout the winter and spring of 1965 and saw *Doctor Who* move from Lime Grove to the comparatively spacious Riverside Studios. Recognising how difficult it must be for O'Brien, who was relatively new to television, to find her place in the established cast and crew, both Jacqueline and William Russell did their best to ensure she felt included. 'She was like a rock,' said O'Brien later. 'You knew that you could completely depend on this person. She was *so* kind to me.'

William Hartnell, too, had come to depend on Jacqueline and Russell; in a context of 'as live' production with virtually no opportunities for retakes, their experience and skill made them invaluable allies on the occasions when he deviated from the script. Hartnell's tendency to forget his lines has sometimes been exaggerated but it did happen from time to time, and even on his better days the reassuring presence of Russell and Jacqueline helped to mitigate tension in the studio with regard to what *might* go wrong. The knock-on effect of a missed cue could be significant enough that even the possibility was stressful, so in a broad sense, everyone involved with making *Doctor Who* benefited from their support of the star.

By the end of April 1965, Jacqueline and William Russell had worked solidly on *Doctor Who* for a year and a half. They had appeared in a total of sixteen serials with settings as diverse as revolutionary Paris, twelfth-century Palestine, the Daleks' home world of Skaro and the jungle planet of Mechanus. This was the point at which they both left the programme.

It was a voluntary departure; by now Verity Lambert had also decided to move on, various other members of the original production team had already left, and both actors had come to feel they'd done enough with their roles. What had begun as something entirely new – a change from the familiar territory of earthbound drama – was now established as routine. 'Everything that we wanted to do in the series had been accomplished and we felt, and I think Verity sneakingly agreed with us, that it was time for the series to try and see if it could do something new. As for the question of going together, well, it all just seemed to come together at the right time for both of us. I think it had always been felt that Ian and Barbara, who had this slightly romantic side to their relationship, should go together much as they came – back to the London they left. They wrote us out well, I thought at the time, and aside from the obvious sentiments, I can't remember having any real regrets.'

Reviewing their final story, *The Chase*, Marjorie Norris wished them well: 'As two of the cast leave of their own wish, it is time to comment on the consistently good quality of their work. No matter how ridiculous the story or (sometimes) poor the dialogue, they have carried off every absurdity without once looking bored. The peculiarities of this space-time marathon made it practically impossible for them or for

William Hartnell (as Dr Who) to develop the characters a great deal. The standard of writing has varied so much that what they have gained on the swings with one they have immediately lost on the roundabouts with another. But when the rare opportunity has arisen it has not been missed.'

*

Jacqueline was aware of fan culture in its pre-internet form, and some of her *Doctor Who* episodes were released on video during her lifetime. In recent decades, though, her work on the programme has had an afterlife on a scale she could never have anticipated.

To begin with, all of the First Doctor's surviving serials have now been commercially released, with the addition of detailed commentary tracks and painstaking animated reconstructions of various episodes missing from the BBC archive. There have been two short documentaries about Jacqueline's life – 1996's *Myth Makers: Jacqueline Hill* (part of a series) and 2011's *A Life in Pictures*. Scripts written for the first TARDIS crew but never produced have been unearthed and published in book form or recorded as audio plays. *Doctor Who Magazine*, which published Richard Marson's interview with Jacqueline in 1985, has evolved into a slick, glossy title in which numerous detailed analyses and behind-the-scenes accounts of the early serials have appeared over the years. A growing body of popular, critical and scholarly writing about the series, ranging from tightly focused academic papers to lavish illustrated books and ambitious multi-volume studies, also encompasses in-depth analyses of those first episodes.

Barbara Wright has had more adventures on the printed page than she ever did on screen, in original *Who* novels, comics and collections of short stories. Spin-off TV series like the early-2000s *Sarah Jane Adventures* and 2016's *Class* have worked passing mentions of Ian and Barbara into their scripts, dropping hints about what became of the characters after their return home. Meanwhile, new material about the original TARDIS crew is still being created in the form of licensed audio plays with Russell, Ford and O'Brien returning in their respective roles; Barbara's dialogue (and the Doctor's; Hartnell died in 1975) is incorporated into the narrative or handled by other cast members. She has also been voiced in some plays by Jemma Powell, who appeared as Jacqueline herself in *An Adventure in Space and Time*. There has never been any question of conveniently writing her out.

All of this has supported an explosion of interest and creativity amongst fans, especially online. As well as official BBC content and material by established series writers and reviewers there are countless in-depth fan review blogs, podcasts, companion appreciation sites, fiction archives and YouTube videos covering what is now called 'Classic Who' as well as the post-2005 'new' show. The tone ranges from good-natured, thoughtful discussion (such as the weekly *Verity!* podcast, named in honour of Lambert) to cheerful silliness (numerous Tumblr blogs on which people slightly too young even to have watched the rebooted programme on its debut, let alone the 1960s version, post long series of black-and-white screenshots captioned with wry, affectionate hashtags).

It's a mixed bag, but at all levels a recurring theme in modern fan conversations about early *Who* is heartfelt appreciation of the quality of performances and depth of characterisation, often stemming from an ever-better understanding of the challenging circumstances in which those early serials were created. Within this context commentators have scrutinised Jacqueline's scenes in detail, assessed Barbara with a feminist gaze, identified her and Ian as the 'moral centre' of the programme. People respond to her intelligence and maturity; they approve of the way she stood up to the Doctor; they celebrate her as a role model, or a #stonecoldbadass, or even a #BAMF.

What might Jacqueline have made of all this? Her direct involvement with fans was limited, and it came at a time when *Who* fandom was a very different place:

smaller, less inclusive, more male-dominated and far less inclined towards critical thinking about the programme's representation of women. Marson's 1985 interview question to her about playing Barbara – 'How easy was it to play the part of such a placid, basically quite quiet woman?' – reads today as if he might have momentarily slipped up and misremembered her as a completely different character; but it would have raised far fewer eyebrows at the time. Her reply, though, is firm. 'I take issue with your label of placidity and quietness. In that particular TARDIS situation, it would have been impossible to be a quiet personality, and I seem to remember that Barbara stood up to the Doctor's know-it-all attitude on occasion. I liked that.'

Following Barbara's departure, Jacqueline had appeared once more in *Doctor Who* (in the 1980 serial *Meglos*, discussed below), and in the spring of 1985 she made her only appearance at a fan-run event. This was a Doctor Who Appreciation Society 'social' held in London; Gordon Roxburgh was the organiser. 'Jacqueline was quite determined prior to the convention, and indeed on the morning when I met her that this would be her one and only convention, and did it to an extent to appease her children (and also probably to stop DWAS and others repeatedly asking her to appear)! The fact that the convention was in Hammersmith was also quite important, as it was close to where she lived, and she was reassured that Carole Ann [Ford] was going to be there as well.' Afterwards, having taken part in a panel discussion and signed some books, she indicated to Roxburgh that she might, after all, be happy to come again. In the end, though, her other commitments made this impossible.

18

'I said to Jackie, "Let's do *Separate Tables*, the
Terence Rattigan play." It was a chance for both
of us and we did a little theatre tour. We weren't
crying to be leaving. I'm always looking forward
to the next experience. You have to as an actor.'

– William Russell

I MMEDIATELY AFTER COMPLETING THEIR run in
Doctor Who, Jacqueline and William Russell
appeared in Terence Rattigan's *Separate Tables* at
the Leeds Grand Theatre. Geoffrey Nethercott, a TV
producer with whom Jacqueline had worked on *The
Executioners* a few years earlier, directed.

In the 1960s it was not always easy for actors to find work after leaving regular television roles. If anything, a strong association with a particular part was sometimes regarded as a disadvantage. But in this instance, the Grand was promoting a 'Television Star Season' and happily billed Jacqueline and Russell as 'Stars of Dr WHO'.

Separate Tables is a pair of one-act plays set in a coastal hotel, and the leading parts in each are written to be played by the same pair of actors. Jacqueline, who had not appeared on stage since *The Shrike* twelve years earlier, may not have been entirely comfortable in her dual leading role. *Yorkshire Post* critic Desmond Pratt gave her a lukewarm review: 'Her Mrs Shankland is too young, but the final reunion is very touching. She does not either fully explore the anguish of the daughter in the second play, although the form is shrivelled and the voice plaintive.'

Apart from one more television part – an episode of *No Hiding Place* called 'You Never Can Tell Till You Try', transmitted in 1966 and now lost – Jacqueline then stepped back from acting for more than a decade. It was a deliberate decision, as she wanted to concentrate on raising her children, Sasha and John, but she may not have anticipated quite how long she would stay away.

'She and Alvin adopted, and I remember it so well,' says Penny Francis. 'We used to have games evenings at their house in Holland Park, and it was a nice time. And then they moved – they decided when Derek and I moved to a big house in Wimbledon that they were going to look for a bigger house too, and they ended up in this glorious house in Bedford Park. Jackie decorated it and made it really beautiful. Half elegant and half comfortable, if you know what I mean. She was in heaven, especially when the babies came. She and Alvin went into a little cocoon with, you know, baby alarms, and they were totally obsessed with these two babies.'

This cocooning stage was no indulgence, but a necessity. The time, space and emotional work needed to help a child settle into an adoptive family – to build attachment without distractions or well-meaning inter-ruptions from family and friends – is significant, and it would have been virtually impossible for Jacqueline to combine parenting with regular television work at this time. During the years that followed, she was protective of her private life and seemed content to stay out of the business.

Ann Davies and her husband, Richard Briers, lived across the road from the Rakoffs and had children of a similar age, so 'there were all sorts of reasons why we became close friends', Davies says. Later in life, she and Jacqueline joined the Open University together. 'Jackie had had to leave school when she was very young, whereas I had stayed until I was eighteen; so when we began the OU I was at more of an advantage than her, and we used to talk over the things she had difficulty with. She worked very hard, and she did very well, until she got ill.

'She didn't talk much about what had happened to her in the past. I don't know if it was because her past was so different from the present, that present when she had her children – or because she was the sort of person who just didn't like to look back. She was very much someone for getting on with things.'

'She adored her children, and that was the focus of her life,' Sheila Hancock says. 'I don't look back and think of her as an ambitious actress, [although] she was very knowledgeable and good at critique, she was very intelligent, and knew about plays. She was very interesting to talk to about plays. You couldn't not be, and be married to Alvin.'

'The rest of life never quite lives up to the time I had with Mum,' recalls John Rakoff. 'I think she gave me everything that she never had . . . Thinking back now, it's all a whirlwind of images: beautiful places, travel, food, her friends – so many friends – the theatre, parties. Mum was always taking me somewhere fabulous. Through all of it, she pushed and moulded me with the education she had craved, and without her I wouldn't be able to hold myself in the way that I do. She taught me how to be comfortable in every world I find myself in. I was a very lucky son.

'If anybody was to ask me what my happiest memory is, it would be sat there in the kitchen watching Mum cook. That run up to the Christmas holidays – she went to town on those preparations, and I would sit there helping in the little ways I could. Every so often she would turn and smile at me and if I was lucky, I'd get to lick a spoon.'

While Sasha and John were still young, Jacqueline and her brother finally reconnected after many years of minimal contact. Following army service in India and elsewhere, Arthur had attended college during the 1950s and then gone into youth work in Yorkshire. In 1960 he married Marjorie Challenger, a physiotherapist; Jacqueline and Alvin sent them a present, but didn't attend the wedding. Arthur and Marjorie went on to have five children, and sometimes they watched Jacqueline in *Doctor Who*. He was proud of his older sister, even if they were not in touch.

The turning point came in 1967. Arthur had attended Lichfield Theological College and was about to be ordained. 'It was such a big step for him to take,' Marjorie says. 'So without telling him, I wrote to Jacqueline and Alvin and invited them to come to the ordination ceremony, which they said they'd love to do. I was delighted. His face was a picture when he saw them.'

From then on, the families grew closer. When the Rakoffs invited Arthur to christen their children, he, Marjorie and their family ('we became known as the Northern cousins') travelled down for the occasion. Later there were visits in both directions, and Jacqueline came to stay on her own once in order to spend time with Arthur. 'As they got to know one another again, they were able to talk everything through. They got much closer, had more in-depth conversations.' Arthur and Marjorie had maintained a degree of contact with great-aunt Rhoda and other surviving Birmingham relatives but, Marjorie says, 'Jackie never would. She wasn't interested, and it's no wonder.'

Once Sasha and John were older, Jacqueline began to think about returning to acting. Davies says, 'I think because of what she had managed to get away from, she wanted to go on doing what it was that had helped her to get away – [being] an actress. She felt that it was an important part of her.' But it proved difficult to pick up the thread of her career. 'She had quite a lot of different things stacked up against her. Even though she had only been in *Doctor Who* for a short period, she'd been very well known in that part, and that caused her problems. At that time, they were more prone not to employ you if you'd been in something like that – they thought everyone would look at you and just see the character you were already known for. I don't think it happens the same way these days. And, of course, they were more inclined not to give you work if you were older. Or if they knew you had children.' It goes without saying that her last two points, at least, relate specifically to women.

Tim Combe, an agent who knew Jacqueline from the early *Doctor Who* days when he'd been an assistant BBC floor manager, offered her representation. But, he says, 'we were concerned that her age would be a factor, and this did prove to be the case. We discussed with her how best to combat it. I think she liked our honesty.' The problem they were grappling with has not gone away; decades later, the relative invisibility of older women on British television remains an issue. Writer Kay Mellor, who began her career working on *Coronation Street* in the 1980s, spoke about it in 2018. 'I was at a conference about women in our industry, and just about every [older] woman in that room had something to say, and most of it was about feeling invisible and saying, "I only ever get to play grandmas. It's never about my life. I'm somebody's mother, girlfriend, it's never about me."'

In 1978, aged forty-nine, Jacqueline was cast in an episode of Granada's courtroom drama series *Crown Court* directed by Richard Martin. Part of the difficulty in coming back was that many of her old contacts had moved on, and newer directors did not know her; but Martin, who had directed several *Doctor Who* serials early in his career, was a familiar face. The episode, 'A Man with Everything', has a strong script by writer and oral historian Tony Parker and an equally strong cast: Anne Reid as 'house mother' of a children's home, Geoffrey Palmer as a wealthy man accused of indecently assaulting a child, Elizabeth Power in a fantastic turn as defence counsel. Joanne Whalley is a teenage witness for the prosecution, and Jacqueline is Palmer's unhappy wife. It is a small role, and squarely within the somebody's-wife zone alluded to by Mellor.

That year she also appeared in Alvin's *Romeo and Juliet*, part of a complete series of 'definitive' BBC Shakespeare adaptations. These were a pet project of the producer Cedric Messina, who made it clear that the directors involved should prioritise traditional production values over what he called 'eccentric interpretations'. Despite the prestige associated with the series, critics and scholars have tended to characterise it as slightly disappointing, and *Romeo and Juliet* was not received with much enthusiasm. The central couple (Patrick Ryecart and Rebecca Saire) do seem oddly matched, although they are surrounded by more experienced performers including John Gielgud as the Chorus and Celia Johnson as Nurse. Jacqueline more than holds her own as a firm but loving Lady Capulet, and it is interesting to see newcomer Alan Rickman playing Tybalt; but it's true that, owing to Messina's stifling brief, there's a sense of something lacking at the production's heart. Reviewing it, Clive James observed, 'Verona seemed to have been built on very level ground, like the floor of a television studio.'

'It was not the happiest production for me,' Alvin says. 'I disliked Cedric Messina, and I'll say so publicly. His method of working was very different to mine. But I think Jackie did a good job, although watching it, you can already see that she is not well. Nobody knew that. Even she didn't know it yet. But she was diagnosed with cancer shortly thereafter.'

When it came, the diagnosis was a cruel blow. 'In those days,' says Sheila Hancock, 'it was a bit of a death sentence.' Afterwards, family life and the management of Jacqueline's health had to take priority over work. Alvin remembers her telling her oncologist very firmly that she demanded at least another ten years for the sake of their children. She continued to act when she could, but never really had the chance to hit her stride again professionally. Whatever energy she might have used to push back against industry ageism and sexism was now more productively channelled into simply staying well.

In 1980 she briefly returned to *Doctor Who*, becoming the first regular companion to reappear as an entirely different character. The programme was now in its eighteenth series, with Tom Baker playing the

Fourth Doctor. As the priestess Lexa in a story called *Meglos* Jacqueline drifts in and out of scenes in flowing robes and a waist-length silver ponytail, delivering uninspired dialogue with her customary dignity before taking a bullet to save the life of the Doctor's companion Romana (Lalla Ward). *Meglos*, widely regarded as a low point of the Baker era, was recorded at Television Centre with Terence Dudley directing. 'Of course, television had moved on in leaps and bounds so that the technique was completely different,' Jacqueline told Richard Marson. 'The special effects were a lot more dominant. It was recorded entirely out of order and there was nobody working on the story who could remember as far back as me – which was something of a humbling experience . . . It was a happy reunion with a show that was really only the same by name.'

There were some similarities, though. When the story was released on DVD many years later (with the documentary *Jacqueline Hill: A Life in Pictures* as an extra), reviewer Gary Gillatt wrote: 'One wonders what the actress made of this trip to a space both strange and familiar. Did she offer Lalla Ward tips on how to act lost in twenty feet of jungle? As a High Priestess plotting a human sacrifice, did Hill recall her finest hour as Barbara, battling to prevent one? . . . Hill's presence short-circuits the first seventeen years of *Doctor Who*, and shows us how little changed over that time.'

Her next part was in BBC medical drama *Angels*, as the long-sought birth mother of a nurse called Vicky (series regular Pauline Quirke). Writer Simon Guerrier watched an archive copy of the episode while researching *A Life in Pictures*. 'It's their first meeting and it doesn't go well, and [Vicky] returns to work never to see her birth mother again. Jackie is never without a cigarette throughout.' The scene accounts for eleven minutes of the half-hour episode. Jacqueline's chain-smoking was in keeping with the overall tone of *Angels*, notable for a level of realism and grit not often seen in earlier, gentler hospital programmes.

Two small roles in Anglia Television's *Tales of the Unexpected* followed. 'The Luncheon' (1983) takes place in the dining room of an expensive London restaurant; Jacqueline steals her scene as an elegant American, unafraid to raise eyebrows with her flirtatious manner. Her part in 1984's 'Accidental Death' as a middle-class widow with a fondness for sherry is even briefer, but crisply funny.

Peter Buckman's *All Together Now* (1986, directed by David Attwood) was the first in BBC2's *Screenplay* strand of experimental short plays. Jacqueline took the role of a tenor horn player in a village brass band; *The Stage* reported that the actors received tutoring in their instruments. Reviewing it, the *Newcastle Journal* suggested that the play and by extension the whole

Screenplay series had been 'tailored too tightly for the box, resulting in stunted growth of events and cramped characterisation'.

In that respect, her final production could hardly have been more different. Directed by Alvin, John Mortimer's ambitious drama *Paradise Postponed* (1986) was a high-profile Euston Films production for Thames Television. Over the course of eleven episodes the series sweeps through thirty years' worth of postwar British history, following characters from a fictional English village; the cast includes Michael Hordern, David Threlfall, Zoe Wanamaker, Jill Bennett and countless other interesting names. Although not without its critics at the time, it remains well regarded today. Writing in the *Guardian* in 2014, Toby Manning called it 'beautifully acted', praising its 'confidence and class'.

Jacqueline plays Mrs Mallard-Greene, a transplanted middle-class Londoner, first seen coming through a downpour with a radiant social smile to take possession of a cottage that really ought to be going to a local family. Before long she is driven to miserable distraction by the loneliness of rural living and the poor life choices of her adolescent son; but eventually the Mallard-Greenes sell up and leave the village, and in the last episode, some of her old polish and confidence is restored. The smile briefly comes back.

It's a slender strand of the overarching story, and the character is not wholly sympathetic, but Jacqueline is excellent: technically assured, emotionally true and a pleasure to watch. Viewing it in the knowledge that this, much too soon, is the final scene of her career, there is an odd mixture of regret and relief at seeing Mrs Mallard-Greene walk out of shot with her head held high, looking well again.

19

'There are certain people that are landmarks in your life, and Jackie certainly was one. These people come along when you need them, I always think. And we came along when we needed one another.'
– Sheila Hancock

Ann Davies

Jackie had two bouts of cancer, and the first was breast cancer, and she fought that very hard, and she dealt with it and she went into remission. She seemed to be fine and she was fine for – for some years. And then she, I don't know whether this triggered it off, but she fell and she cracked her sternum. And after she had recovered from the actual sort of break, it was discovered that she had bone cancer. And again, she fought it like mad, she fought it like anything.

Sheila Hancock

We didn't meet again at all [after RADA] until we both ended up at Bristol Cancer Centre. I think we spent a week there. It was a terrific experience. I don't know if Jackie had just been diagnosed, but I certainly had, and in those days . . . it was a bit of a death sentence. It was before all those wonderful drugs which have now made life expectancy hugely better than when we were there. So we were badly in need of comfort and support, and the Bristol Cancer Centre gave it, par excellence. It's grown hugely since then, it's a big organisation, but then, it was one house, and you got to know people.

I remember we were slightly belligerent while we were there, I remember we got a bit pissed off with all the loveliness, and you know, if you think lovely thoughts you'll be cured, kind of thing. And I remember one particular art class where we were supposed to say how we saw our cancer, and I just did a black thing, just all black, a whole page of black – and there was a tiny drop of yellow paint on it. I think it was an accident, but anyway, there it was. And I remember the woman interpreting it as, 'Ah, there's light at the end of the tunnel', kind of thing, and I remember being absolutely livid and saying to Jackie, no it isn't any bloody light at the end of the tunnel. So we were slightly a nuisance, I think, the two of us, while we were there, with those sort of things.

But on the other hand there were some amazing people there. There was a wonderful healer – Michael Pilkington, and he was a wonderful man and hugely comforting and you did really feel, when you had a session with him, that probably you had a hope. We ate very sensibly there, and between us, we came out much better. And then we became very friendly after that, because we lived locally, so we kept in touch.

Because when you have something like cancer, it's very difficult for people who haven't got it to understand how you feel. It's rather like bereavement – it's like any experience in life, it's always easier to share what you're feeling with somebody who comes from the same point as you, you know? So we used to meet on a regular basis, and cheer one another up, and encourage one another, and all that.

There are some people when they die, after a while, you lose the image of them, do you know what I mean? You can remember things about them, things that they did and said, but you can't conjure up a very clear visual image of them. And Jackie's one of those people that you can. She was such a strong presence. I mean, I can see her in front of me now. And there was something about her, I mean – we laughed a lot, we laughed a lot together, but I also did lean on her quite a bit, because she was immensely strong. And you know, the fact that her children were adopted – you know, somebody that does that, there's something special and positive about them. She was positive. A very positive woman.

It always annoys me when people say how lovely dead people were. I mean, they go on about it. But certainly, my experience – my memory of her is really all good. I can't think of anything that irritated me about her. I loved seeing her. It was a huge help to me when we got together. And I hope, maybe, it was vice versa, that we supported one another.

And we could talk. I mean, one of the other things about the Bristol cure was to look back at your past and to find things that were troubling you, and to try and get rid of them in your life. If there were things that were wrong, in your life, then it was best not to nag on and worry about them, but to do something about them, and between us, we discussed quite serious things that were happening in our private lives, which I'm not going to discuss with you, but they were quite personal and serious. And I think, probably, that she was one of the only people that I discussed those with; and I think vice versa.

We really were a terrible nuisance [at Bristol]. We kept being very cynical, which – it was in a period when everything was very new-age-y, you know, and there were all sorts of enlightenment groups going on, and funny things that you went to for a weekend and you came out with your life solved – not just with cancer, but a general movement that was happening at that period. Both of us found it hugely irritating, that you could solve your life with a week of talk, you know, and also this romantic version that everything was going to be all right. When patently obviously, at Bristol, where there were some people who were *really* ill, it wasn't all right. It was bloody difficult to find any positive thing.

I mean, bless their hearts, that's what they were there to do, to help us be positive. But we fought against it quite a bit. Although, having said that, we did come out feeling much more positive, so you know, it achieved its objective. But in the process, we were probably more challenging than most people would be. Partly because we were both actors, therefore we spoke up. We weren't frightened of the sound of our own voices. We were used to participating, and talking emotionally, which is what you do in rehearsal. It wasn't as new to us as some of the people that were there who had never spoken up for themselves. I remember it being quite [a] small [group], and one got quite close to an awful lot of them, one was very distressed for some of them as well, you know.

I think both of us were trying to do too much in our lives. I think we both came out with the courage – which we supported one another in – to do less for everybody.

She was an extraordinarily well-rounded woman. She was *a woman*. She was strong, and even under the circumstances, when both of us were shit scared – she was nevertheless strong, and supportive of me, and everybody. It was amazing that I met her at Bristol, because I didn't know she was going to be there, and we sort of fell upon one another because we recognised one another in the initiation meeting, and it was such a relief to see somebody that I could relate to, and that feeling remained for me, that I could relate to her – and that was immensely valuable.

There are certain people that are landmarks in your life, and Jackie certainly was one. These people come along when you need them, I always think. And we came along when we needed one another. Sadly it was only for that period, but it was immensely important.

Penny Francis

I realised how ill she was when we were at the National Portrait Gallery, and I realised she couldn't even walk around the foyer.

She was really far gone, at that stage. It was in her bones, and it was – it was awful. It was really awful.

Ann Davies

She used to have to go to Charing Cross Hospital, and I think she was having chemotherapy, and she used to sit there and they used to put – like a bathing hat on her head. This was to try and prevent the loss of hair. And they used to put various liquids through tubes that circulated round the head – the hat. It really did look like a rather convoluted bathing hat. I used to go with her and we used to sit together, and it used to take, I don't know, an hour, an hour and a half? It was quite a process. And then afterwards she used to have to have her hair washed, and there – she couldn't do it herself, and there wasn't really any nurse available, so I used to wash it for her, in this basin. And it was a lovely quiet room. There was something very peaceful about it, and there would be about three people having various things like that done, and – it's a funny thing to say, but they really were lovely times. There was just something between us, and – I felt very close to her then. Very close.

William Russell

I now know why we didn't see so much of Jackie before she died, because she was changing so much with the disease. It was awful but she was really stricken and didn't want to see us. I was always ringing her up and saying, 'Come to this or that' but there was always an excuse. And then when I spoke to Alvin, he said she'd changed so much with the cancer and just didn't want to see people.

Alvin Rakoff

She was determined to survive, she was determined to live as long as she could. She did psychologically prepare herself, as much as anyone can, for, for – her demise. I've said before, watching Jackie become iller and iller was one of the bravest things I've seen in any human being, ever; and I've seen a reasonable amount of bravery in my life. She was extraordinary. She kept going, as long as she could . . . and that was that.

Watching someone you love dwindle because of cancer – someone as strong and loving a personality as Jackie was – watching them go is not easy.

Ann Davies

The funny thing is, because we live opposite each other, and I used to go out and sometimes I'd see her coming out of her front door as well, and we'd both be going shopping – not necessarily at the same places, or together, or anything – and sometimes I step out there, and I still think I might see her. It's a very strange feeling. And Alvin had a tree put on the green in her memory, and I sometimes go and walk past that and have a chat with her.

My really biggest memory of her is what a wonderful, marvellous friend she was. She was a really terrific friend to me, through thick and thin. And that's how I remember her.

20

J ACQUELINE DIED ON 18 February 1993, at sixty-three years old. Her younger brother, Arthur, had predeceased her several years earlier.

Sheila Hancock spoke at her memorial service. 'I didn't feel that I knew Jackie as much as some other people,' she says, 'but I did feel her loss hugely. She meant a lot to me, and was such a support to me.' She pauses. 'But I think I mainly talked about how funny she was at the Bristol Cancer Centre.'

Obituaries appeared in *The Stage* and various newspapers, tracing her career in some depth. At home, though, it was the painful loss of a mother, wife and close friend that really mattered, and her family's grief was intense. Even – or especially – after her prolonged illness, coming to terms with Jacqueline's death was a complicated, private process for the people left behind.

*

While I was researching this book I came across the term 'ghost texts', which the television historian Jason Jacobs has used to describe lost works of early TV drama. Ghost texts are productions of which there is no archive recording, but which 'exist instead as shadows, dispersed and refracted amongst buried files, bad memories, a flotsam of fragments'. Jacobs tries to piece some of these written fragments together, as a way of partially reconstituting audio-visual material that can never be seen again.

His description stayed with me as I gathered inform-ation about Jacqueline's early life; it seemed to apply not only to her work, but to many aspects of her story. Nobody I spoke with knew (because she herself had not known) the details of her mother's life or death; the shadowy, faulty memories she found so frustrating were, you might say, ghost traces of that lost relationship. Equally, nobody was sure about the circumstances of her father's fatal accident, only that he'd been on his bicycle at the time. Information about her years at Bournville was sketchy and there was no record of which scholarship she'd won to RADA, no family story of how she'd learned about it in the first place. She had kept some old press cuttings, but she was disinclined to make much fuss about her own achievements. For the most part, everything that had happened in her working life before she met Alvin – meeting Sam Wanamaker, the break into television with *Shop Window*, the excitement of shooting *The Blue Parrot* – had dropped out of living memory, and had to be reconstructed from archives.

Clearly, there were aspects that could never be reanimated. At the heart of things, Jacqueline's own take on all of it – her impressions and opinions, her private version of the story – remained elusive.

What did become apparent, though, is that no matter what the *Evening Standard* said, television didn't really 'create a future' for her; she did that herself. From an early age, in a society that largely discouraged ambition in working-class girls, she was able to imagine a life more fulfilling and more emotionally secure than the one she knew. Making her way towards it, she managed grief and disappointment, navigated practical obstacles and learned the ropes of a dynamic, technically demanding new industry, all without losing sight of what mattered.

Those who knew Jacqueline talk about her skill as a performer, her work ethic and strong collaborative spirit; they also remember her resilience, generosity, humour and kindness. All of these qualities came into play as she built her career and raised her family. One powerful five-minute television appearance marked an important turn on her path; but the credit for the rest belongs to her.

Afterword

THERE WERE LOTS OF ACTRESSES on BBC1 on the
night of 23 November 1963. After Jacqueline
Hill had taken her first journey into time and
space, Anna Quayle popped up on *Juke Box Jury*, Anne
Ridler was in the middle of her regular run as WP Sgt
Freeman in *Dixon of Dock Green*, Elsie and Doris Waters
were in a Jack Rosenthal-penned *Comedy Playhouse*
and Millicent Martin sang on *That Was The Week That
Was*. Fine performers all, with careers to be proud of.

It's sobering just how many well-known people and
shows made up that random BBC Saturday night all
those years ago; all of those programmes are important
parts of TV history in some way, all of those performers

made their mark on their industry. It's fair to say though, the programme that probably seemed the least remarkable at the time, what looked to most like a disposable early-evening children's science-fiction show, is the one broadcast on that cold November night that has been watched the most and has had the most words written about it.

At the time Jacqueline Hill would have had no idea that the performance she was about to give would be scrutinised over and over again, repeated over the years, commercially released in various forms, the subject of documentaries, and even partially restaged fifty years later for a high-profile celebratory TV film.

So it's a good job she's so brilliant in it.

And she is; I remember having the episode on with a former partner (no mean actress herself) who said, 'Bloody hell – she's really good' (she hadn't, I think, expected to find much to her taste from the ancient science-fiction adored by her geeky beau). Time isn't always kind to acting styles, but Jacqueline Hill's performance is so true, so nuanced, so honest that – appropriately – it defies the passage of time.

Acting can be quite a cruel mistress. Most performers have to give the profession much more than they get out of it. Thanks to *Doctor Who*, though, anyone who has run up and down its corridors will continue to be appreciated as fans watch and rewatch, assess and reassess its episodes. And because of that, Jacqueline Hill's brilliance, her professionalism, her truthfulness, will continue to be enjoyed for years to come.

That's time travel.

Toby Hadoke
January 2020

Sources

NEWSPAPERS (CITED IN **Notes**) were consulted at the British Library, the Dudley Archives Centre and the National Library of Scotland as well as online via the British Newspaper Archive. Other archive material used in the text comes from the BBC Written Archives Centre, Caversham (© BBC, with permission); Cadbury's, Bournville; the RADA Library, London; the V&A Theatre and Performance Archives, London; the Wolfson Centre for Archival Research, Birmingham Library; the online British Library Theatre Archive Project; and the Hill/Rakoff family's personal archive. Viewing of *The Chopping Block*, *The Fixers* and *Maigret* was arranged through the British Film Institute and Scottish Screen.

Thomas Guerrier and Simon Guerrier generously shared footage of their interviews with Alvin Rakoff and Ann Davies (thanks in particular to Thomas for persevering with a technically challenging conversion process). My own conversations with Alvin, Ann, Marjorie Hill, Penny Francis, Sheila Hancock, Tony Britton, Jennifer Phipps and others took place during the period 2013–17.

Baily, Kenneth (ed.), *The Television Annual for 1953* (London: Odhams, 1952).

Baily, Kenneth (ed.), *The Television Annual for 1954* (London: Odhams, 1953).

Baily, Kenneth (ed.), *The Television Annual for 1955* (London: Odhams, 1954).

Baily, Kenneth (ed.), *The Television Annual for 1956* (London: Odhams, 1955).

Baily, Kenneth (ed.), *The Television Annual for 1957* (London: Odhams, 1956).

Baily, Kenneth (ed.), *The Television Annual for 1958* (London: Odhams, 1957).

Baily, Kenneth (ed.), *The Television Annual for 1959* (London: Odhams, 1958).

Baily, Kenneth (ed.), *The Television Annual for 1960* (London: Odhams, 1959).

Baily, Kenneth (ed.), *The Television Annual for 1961* (London: Odhams, 1960).

Barnes, Kenneth R., *Welcome, Good Friends* (London: P. Davis, 1958).

Bishop, Harold, 'Twenty-five years of BBC television', *BBC Engineering Division Monograph No 39*: October 1961, https://www.bbceng.info/ Technical%20Reviews/early_colour_tv.htm (last accessed 14 July 2019).

Bournville Utilities: A War Record (Birmingham: Bournville Utilities Ltd., 1945).

Bray, Christopher, *Sean Connery: The Measure of a Man* (London: Faber, 2010).

Cadbury, Deborah, *Chocolate Wars* (London: HarperCollins, 2010).

Chibnall, Steve, and Brian McFarlane, *The British B Film* (London: BFI, 2009).

Curtis, Jo-Ann, 'Cadbury's Angels and World War One', http://www.suburbanbirmingham.org.uk (last accessed 22 March 2014).

Doctor Who: The Chase DVD commentary track (2entertain, 2010).

Doctor Who: Origins, documentary, prod. Richard Molesworth (2Entertain, 2006).

Dunn, Kate, *Do Not Adjust Your Set* (London: John Murray, 2003).

Eddington, Paul, *So Far, So Good* (London: Hodder, 1996).

Fairley, Roma, *The Small Screen* (London: Cassell & Co., 1958).

Finch, John, *Granada Television: The First Generation* (Manchester: Manchester University Press, 2003).

Freeman, Gwendolen, *The Houses Behind* (London: George Allen and Unwin, 1947).

Future Memories: Making 'The Dalek Invasion of Earth', documentary, prod. Peter Finklestone (2entertain, 2003).

Hewett, Richard, *The Changing Spaces of Television Acting* (Manchester: Manchester University Press, 2017).

Jacobs, Jason, *The Intimate Screen* (Oxford: Oxford University Press, 2000).

Jacqueline Hill: A Life in Pictures, documentary, prod. Thomas Guerrier (2entertain, 2011).

James, Clive, *Clive James on Television* (London: Picador, 1991).

Kershaw, Baz (ed.), *The Cambridge History of British Theatre Vol. 3* (Cambridge: Cambridge University Press, 2004).

Kynaston, David, *Family Britain* (London: Bloomsbury, 2009).

Last Stop White City, documentary, prod. James Goss (2entertain, 2006).

Marson, Richard, interview with Jacqueline Hill, *Doctor Who Magazine* no. 105, October 1985.

Miller, Mary Jane: *Turn Up the Contrast: CBC Television Drama since 1952* (Vancouver: University of British Columbia Press, 1987).

Moran, Joe, *Armchair Nation* (London: Profile Books, 2014).

Plummer, Gillian, *Failing Working-Class Girls* (London: UCL Institute of Education Press, 2000).

Potter, Ian, *The Rise and Rise of the Independents* (London: Guerilla Books, 2008).

Sellers, Robert, *Don't Let the Bastards Grind You Down* (London: Arrow, 2012).

Sellers, Robert, *Peter O'Toole: The Definitive Biography* (London: Sidgwick & Jackson, 2015).

Shearman, Robert, and Toby Hadoke, *Running Through Corridors Vol. 1: The 60s* (Des Moines: Mad Norwegian Press, 2010).

Shellard, Dominic, *The Golden Generation: New Light on Post-War British Theatre* (London: British Library Publishing, 2008).

Shubik, Irene, *Play for Today: The Evolution of Television Drama* (Manchester: Manchester University Press, 2001).

Thumim, Janet, *Inventing Television Culture: Men, Women, and the Box* (Oxford: Oxford University Press, 2004).

Vague, Tom, *Notting Hill History*,
     http://www.vaguerants.org.uk/wp-content/
     uploads/2010/06/timelinechap7.pdf (last accessed
     22 March 2014).

Wake, Oliver, '*Out of this World* (1962)',
     http://www.britishtelevisiondrama.org.uk/?p=213
     (last accessed 16 September 2018).

Weedall, Albert, *Bournville College of Further
     Education: 75 Years of Continuity and Change*
     (Birmingham: Bournville College, 1989).

Williams, Raymond, *Television: Technology and
     Cultural Form* (Abingdon-on-Thames: Routledge,
     2003).

Chronology

[1946]	[Bournville DCS Drama Group]	*[Twelfth Night]*
1947	Bournville DCS Drama Group	*Pride and Prejudice*
1947	Bournville Dramatic Society	*The Doctor's Duty*
1947	Bournville Dramatic Society	*Mr Bolfry*
1948	Bournville DCS Drama Group	*Pygmalion*
1948	Bournville Youths' Club	*The Bracelet*
1948	Bournville Dramatic Society	*Sweeney Todd*
1949	Bournville DCS Drama Group	*The Barretts of Wimpole Street*

1951	RADA	*RADA Public Show*, New Theatre (Noël Coward Theatre)
1953	Princes Theatre (Shaftesbury Theatre)	*The Shrike*
1953	BBC	*Shop Window*
1953	ACT Films	*The Blue Parrot*
1953	BBC	*The Rose and the Ring*
1954	BBC	*Teleclub*
[1954]	[BBC]	*[Fabian of the Yard]*
1955	BBC	*The Legend of Pepito*
1955	BBC	*A Business of His Own*
1955	BBC	*Three Empty Rooms*
1956	BBC	*The Seat of the Scornful*
1956	ITV	*Martine*
1957	BBC	*Requiem for a Heavyweight*
1957	BBC	*Joyous Errand*
1957	BBC	*Her Affairs in Order*
1958	ITV	*Man in the Corner*
1958	ITV	*Poet's Corner*
1958	ITV	*The Curious Savage*
1959	ITV	*The Flying Doctor:* 'Brainstorm'
1959	BBC	*The Velvet Alley*
1960	BBC	*The Man Who Came to Dinner*
1960	BBC	*The Chopping Block*
1961	BBC	*The Watching Cat*
1961	ITV	*The Executioners*
1961	BBC	*The Men from Room 13:* 'The Man Who Made Trouble'
1962	BBC	*Six Proud Walkers*
1962	ITV	*No Hiding Place:* 'The Bank Job'
1962	ITV	*Out of This World:* 'Medicine Show'
1962	Grayfilms/Consort	*The Comedy Man*
1962	BBC	*Maigret:* 'The Trap'

1963	ITV	*The Fixers*
1963– 1965	BBC	*Doctor Who*
1965	Leeds Grand Theatre	*Separate Tables*
1966	ITV	*No Hiding Place:* 'You Never Can Tell Till You Try'
1978	ITV	*Crown Court:* 'A Man with Everything'
1978	BBC	*Romeo and Juliet*
1980	BBC	*Doctor Who: Meglos*
1983	ITV	*Tales of the Unexpected:* 'The Luncheon'
1984	ITV	*Tales of the Unexpected:* 'Accidental Death'
1986	BBC	*All Together Now*
1986	BBC	*Paradise Postponed*

Acknowledgements

THIS SHORT BOOK has taken a long time to write, and many people have helped along the way.

The initial spark came from Simon Guerrier. All Simon's ideas are excellent, but this one would never have come to anything without his patient encouragement and really astonishing generosity with his time – not only at the start, but at many stages throughout. I'm extremely grateful to him, as well as to Debbie Challis and their family.

Alvin Rakoff has been candid, gracious and helpful, and thanks to him I was able to make contact with a number of other interviewees. Conversations with Marjorie Hill were immensely useful in laying the foundation for the book, not least by identifying gaps in family knowledge that would need to be bridged with research. Both Alvin and Marjorie were kind enough to trust me with photos and personal documents. My thanks also go to Sasha Rakoff and John Rakoff for their acknowledgement of the project and willingness to let it go ahead.

Meeting Penny Francis was a privilege, and in the course of a single afternoon she contributed perhaps more than anyone to my sense of Jacqueline as a living, laughing presence. Sheila Hancock's recollections of time spent at the Bristol Cancer Centre were so engaging that I could hardly bear to edit them; I hope she will not mind being quoted verbatim and at length. Conversations with Ann Davies and the late Jennifer Phipps also reinforced the impression that Jacqueline had a strong instinct for making friends with wonderful people.

A number of friendly contacts gave valuable advice (so long ago now that they may have forgotten all about it). Among them, Rob Baker passed on information about 1950s London, Louis Barfe shared insights about Henry Caldwell and BBC light entertainment, and Melanie Williams took the time to consider parallels between *The Chopping Block* and *Woman in a Dressing Gown*. Thanks also to Justin Lewis for book recommendations, encouragement and kindness.

Thank you to David Barry, Tony Britton, Janet Carter, Tim Combe, Thomas Guerrier and Hilary Wood; and to Dexter O'Neill at Fantom, typesetter Phil Reynolds, Ed Padmore and Sarune Kalininaite at Vintage Photo Lab, James Thornton at RADA and Robert Witts at Coventry History Centre. Thanks to David J. Howe for liaising with the estates of Raymond Cusick and Barry Newbery for permission to use their *Doctor Who* production photographs. Thanks also to staff at the BBC Written Archives Centre, the BFI research viewing service, the Birmingham Library, the British Library, Cadbury's archive at Bournville, Dudley Archives, the National Library of Scotland and the V&A Theatre and Performance Archive.

Closer to home, a number of people have been supportive and made life brighter, often while listening patiently to me ramble about the contents of this book: my mother, Carolyn; Nick; Adam and Phoebe; Peggy; Laura; Anna and Cris, whose offer of precious space to write restarted a stalled process; and John, who is the most perceptive reader imaginable, and much more besides.

Notes

Prologue

1   At mid-morning . . . This account draws on the inquest report
relating to the death of Morris B. Roberts, 8 August 1930, held
at the Library of Birmingham. His death was also reported in
the *Birmingham Daily Gazette* ('Killed on railway', 8 August
1930, p. 7; 'Decapitated on railway', 9 August 1930, p. 4). In
some sources, his name is spelled 'Maurice'.

1   cool and showery . . . 'The weather', *Birmingham Daily Gazette*,
7 August 1930, p. 7.

Chapter 1

5   'We drove up to Birmingham' . . . Conversation with Alvin
Rakoff, 2014.

7   'a bit of a thespian' . . . Conversation with Marjorie Hill, 2013.

7   lived on Dale Road . . . Midlands Electoral Registers, 1935
     onwards; *County Express*, 11 September 1937; *County Express*, 9
     October 1937.

8   saw each other regularly . . . *County Express*, 11 September 1937.

9   'The 'bus driver' . . . *County Express*, 9 October 1937.

9   'taken their lives in their hands' . . . *County Express*, 9 October
     1937.

9   'Mrs Grace Maud Hill' . . . *County Express*, 9 October 1937.

10   on parish relief . . . Conversation with Marjorie Hill, 2013.

10   informally adopt them . . . Conversation with Marjorie Hill,
     2013.

10   'a sort of vague apparition' . . . Conversation with Alvin Rakoff,
     2014.

11   'without any friends' . . . Conversation with Marjorie Hill, 2013.

11   'a tyrant' . . . Conversation with Alvin Rakoff, 2014.

12   'they were together' . . . Conversation with Alvin Rakoff, 2014.

13   'the most frightening night' . . . See
     <http://www.bbc.co.uk/history/ww2peopleswar/stories/42/a360
     8642.shtml> (last accessed 23 June 2019).

13   'bits of anti-aircraft shells' . . . See
     <http://www.bbc.co.uk/history/ww2peopleswar/stories/71/a417
     5471.shtml> (last accessed 23 June 2019).

13   'top of the class' . . . See
     <http://www.swanshurst.org/barra/record.asp?recordid=4156>
     (last accessed 30 June 2013).

14   did not really need an education . . . See Gillian Plummer,
     Failing Working-Class Girls.

Chapter 2

15   'I wasn't going to let' . . . Jacqueline Hill interviewed in *Doctor
     Who Magazine*, October 1985.

15   light and airy . . . See Jo-Ann Curtis, 'Cadbury's Angels'.

16   bar on the employment . . . See Jo-Ann Curtis, 'Cadbury's Angels'.

16   the most striking changes . . . Deborah Cadbury, *Chocolate Wars*, pp. 259–60.

17   two thousand people . . . Bournville Utilities Ltd., *Bournville Utilities: A War Record*.

17   'a new kind of Assortment Box' . . . Bournville Utilities Ltd., *Bournville Utilities: A War Record*, pp. 24, 25.

17   Day Continuation School . . . Albert Weedall, *Bournville College of Further Education*, p. 42.

18   'to many a girl the most exciting lesson' . . . *BDCS Magazine*, July 1948, p. 9.

18   'a delightful one in every way' . . . *Our Link*, July 1946, n.p.

19   'the rare gift' . . . *BDCS Magazine*, July 1948, p. 10.

19   'A5r invited us all to a party' . . . *Our Link*, September 1947, p. 81.

20   'The production is a joy' . . . *Birmingham Gazette* review reproduced in *Our Link*, September 1947, p. 81.

20   'All classes of employees take part' . . . Great Britain Board of Education, 'Drama in adult education', p. 9, quoted in *The Cambridge History of British Theatre*, p. 134.

21   'The BDS need not fear' . . . *Bournville Works Magazine*, December 1947, n.p.

21   'a typist and teapot-carrier' . . . James Bridie, *Mr Bolfry*, scene one.

22   'This is a difficult play' . . . *Bournville Works Magazine*, February 1948, p. 36.

22   'outstanding' . . . *Bournville Works Magazine*, July 1948, p. 151.

22   'J. Hill, Friday' . . . *Our Link*, July 1948, p. 1 and p. 9.

23   'an admirably restrained Elizabeth Barrett' . . . *Bournville Works Magazine*, March 1949, p. 60.

24   'He gets so excited' . . . Rudolf Besier, *The Barretts of Wimpole Street*, Act II.

24   'Elizabeth picks up Flush' . . . Besier, *The Barretts of Wimpole Street*, Act V.

24   'The setting was a little too attractive' . . . *Bournville Works Magazine*, March 1949, p. 60.

24   'the charming voice of Jacqueline Hill' . . . *Our Link*, July 1949, p. 104.

24   'sort of the next shelf up' . . . Thelma Barlow, Theatre Archive Project interview transcript <http://sounds.bl.uk/related-content/TRANSCRIPTS/024T-C1142X000105-ZZZZA0.pdf> (last accessed 23 June 2019).

24   'walk on occasionally at the Rep' . . . 'Voice two continents like', *Birmingham Mail*, 6 May 1958, p. 3.

25   'They had nothing at home' . . . Conversation with Marjorie Hill, 2013.

25   'They were very ordinary people' . . . Conversation with Marjorie Hill, 2013.

26   'I had set my heart' . . . Jacqueline Hill interviewed in *Doctor Who Magazine*, October 1985.

26   British Theatre Exhibition . . . Details of this event draw upon newspaper reports including 'British theatre display', *The Times*, 18 March 1949, p. 6; 'Theatre exhibition at Bingley Hall', *Birmingham Post*, 23 May 1949, p. 1; 'Visitors amazed by theatre exhibition', *Birmingham Post*, 26 May 1949, p. 1.

26   Baird portable television receiver . . . 'Novel item at exhibition', *Birmingham Post*, 3 June 1949.

26   'My first real opportunity came by chance' . . . 'Voice two continents like', *Birmingham Mail*, 6 May 1958, p. 3.

27   a typical audition of the period . . . Kenneth R. Barnes, *Welcome, Good Friends*, p. 139.

28   called back later for a second audition . . . Email conversation with Hilary Wood, 2014.

Chapter 3

29   'She had truth on her side' . . . Correspondence with Jennifer Phipps, May 2013.

29　'no different from any other university school' . . . '"Cowboy" Al is swotting Shaw', *Daily Mail*, 2 December 1949, p. 4.

29　'I could not have gone' . . . 'Voice two continents like', *Birmingham Mail*, 6 May 1958, p. 3.

30　'She was what we called "finals"' . . . Conversation with Sheila Hancock, May 2013.

30　'the R-A-D-A' . . . Peter Bartlett, Theatre Archive Project interview transcript, <http://sounds.bl.uk/related-content/TRANSCRIPTS/024T-1CDR0032960X-0100A0.pdf> (last accessed 23 June 2019).

31　'a terrible old snob' . . . Quoted at <http://www.janenightwork.com/recollections/the-rada/> (last accessed 30 June 2013).

31　'he was getting somewhat senile' . . . Quoted in Robert Sellers, *Don't Let the Bastards Grind You Down*, p. 46.

31　'RADA students of the Barnes era' . . . Following Sir Kenneth's retirement, director John Fernald took over the position and swiftly began to modernise the course.

31　'a quotation from the Old Testament' . . . Paul Eddington, *So Far, So Good*, p. 75.

31　rapid-fire practice of tongue twisters . . . See Eddington, *So Far, So Good*, p. 76.

32　tended to divide opinion . . . See Eddington, *So Far, So Good*, p. 77, and Robert Sellers, *Peter O'Toole: The Definitive Biography*, n.p.

32　'no-one ever played the whole of a leading part' . . . Quoted at <http://www.janenightwork.com/recollections/the-rada/> (last accessed 30 June 2013).

32　'She was my greatest friend' . . . Correspondence with Jennifer Phipps, 2014.

33　'She loved RADA' . . . Conversation with Alvin Rakoff, March 2014.

33　'The Public Show' . . . Kenneth R. Barnes, *Welcome, Good Friends*, pp. 131–2.

34 'The rest got variations on "Your carriage awaits"' . . . Quoted at
   <http://www.janenightwork.com/recollections/the-rada/> (last
   accessed 30 June 2013).

34 'camping around the stage' . . . Eddington, *So Far, So Good*, p.
   77.

34 'just the kind of play needed' . . . 'RADA matinee', *The Times*, 14
   March 1951, p. 2.

34 'that delightful scene' . . . 'London theatres: The New: RADA
   matinee', *The Stage*, 15 March 1951, p. 10.

Chapter 4

36 'I'd heard that Sam Wanamaker was auditioning' . . . 'Out of the
   Window', *Lilliput* vol. 33, no. 3, issue 195 (August–September
   1953), p. 32.

37 'Jack Hylton and Sam Wanamaker have arranged' . . . 'Chit
   Chat', *The Stage*, 11 December 1952.

37 'In my opinion, it is necessary' . . . 'Truth and theatricality', *The
   Stage*, 17 April 1952, p. 1.

39 'the "unimportant" play' . . . 'Personality and truth', *The Stage*,
   26 February 1953, p. 10.

39 'You learn a lot [in rep]' . . . 'Out of the Window', *Lilliput* vol.
   33, no. 3, issue 195 (August–September 1953), p. 32.

39 'I started round the agencies' . . . 'Out of the Window', *Lilliput*,
   p. 32.

40 'I'd heard that Sam Wanamaker was auditioning' . . . 'Out of the
   Window', *Lilliput*, p. 32.

40 'Howard Bay's settings' . . . 'London Theatres: Brighton
   premiere', *The Stage*, 22 January 1953, p. 10.

41 London critics praised . . . See *Telegraph* and *Express* cuttings
   held in JH file, V&A Theatre Archive, n.d.; 'Princes Theatre: The
   Shrike', *The Times*, 14 February 1953, p. 8; 'The tortures of
   psychiatry', *Kensington Post*, 20 February 1953.

Chapter 5

42 'The five minutes that changed' . . . 'Five minutes that changed her future', *Evening Standard*, 22 June 1953.

43 'Dear Mr Wanamaker' . . . Letter, Holland Bennett to Sam Wanamaker, 12 March 1953 (BBC WAC, Sam Wanamaker file).

44 'great and popular artists of the future' . . . *Shop Window* draft press release, 13 March 1952 (BBC WAC, *Shop Window* file 1: T12/352/1).

44 'series of "discoveries"' . . . *Shop Window* draft press release, 13 March 1952 (BBC WAC, *Shop Window* file 1: T12/352/1).

45 'I am very anxious' . . . Memo, Henry Caldwell to Cecil McGivern, 12 November 1951 (BBC WAC, *Shop Window* file 1: T12/352/1).

45 'Almost the entire cast' . . . Memo, Henry Caldwell to H. Tel. L.E., 11 February 1952 (BBC WAC, *Shop Window* file 1: T12/352/1).

46 'This programme takes you' . . . Memo, Cecil McGivern to Henry Caldwell, 11 March 1952 (BBC WAC, *Shop Window* file 1: T12/352/1).

46 'enthusiasm and wish to co-operate' . . . Memo, Michael Barry to Cecil McGivern, 13 March 1952 (BBC WAC, *Shop Window* file 1: T12/352/1).

47 'insufficient' . . . Memo, Holland Bennett to Cecil McGivern, 10 October 1952 (BBC WAC, *Shop Window* file 1: T12/352/1).

47 'free-for-all' . . . Memo, Henry Caldwell to Ronald Waldman, 15 June 1953 (BBC WAC, *Shop Window* file 2: T12/352/2).

47 'some people had *two teas*' . . . Memo, Humphreys to Henry Caldwell, 31 July 1953 (BBC WAC, *Shop Window* file 2: T12/352/2).

47 'the largest sheet of glass' . . . Memo, Roy Oxley to Ronald Waldman, 20 November 1952 (BBC WAC, *Shop Window* file 2: T12/352/2).

47 'Many congratulations to you' . . . Memo, Cecil McGivern to Henry Caldwell, 21 April 1953 (BBC WAC, *Shop Window* file 2: T12/352/2).

47 'While doing everything in our power' . . . Memo, Cecil McGivern to H. D&S.Tel., 21 April 1953 (BBC WAC, *Shop Window* file 2: T12/352/2).

47 'This was brilliant television' . . . Memo, Cecil McGivern to Ronald Waldman, 19 May 1953 (BBC WAC, *Shop Window* file 2: T12/352/2).

49 'a complicated detailed rehearsal' . . . Memo, Henry Caldwell to Ronald Waldman, 15 June 1953 (BBC WAC, *Shop Window* file 2: T12/352/2).

50 'It's a scene from *Golden Boy*' . . . Roma Fairley, *The Small Screen*, p. 41. The author and publishers have been unable to trace a copyright-holder for this title (published by Cassell & Co. in 1958), and would be grateful for information that might help in doing so.

51 'At the first rehearsal' . . . 'Out of the Window', *Lilliput*, p. 32.

52 'How can a show be put on' . . . Memo, Henry Caldwell to Ronald Waldman, 15 June 1953 (BBC WAC, *Shop Window* file 2: T12/352/2).

52 'It is obvious from the beginning' . . . Roma Fairley, *The Small Screen*, pp. 64–5. The author and publishers have been unable to trace a copyright-holder for this title (published by Cassell & Co. in 1958), and would be grateful for information that might help in doing so.

53 'We pitched our performances' . . . Quoted in Kate Dunn, *Do Not Adjust Your Set*, p. 59.

54 'Sam is such a wonderful actor' . . . 'Out of the Window', *Lilliput*, p. 32.

Chapter 6

56 'On the morning after' . . . 'Out of the Window', *Lilliput* vol. 33, no. 3, issue 195 (August–September 1953), p. 32.

57 'That Tuesday morning' . . . 'Five minutes that changed her future', *Evening Standard*, 22 June 1953.

58 'More, and more easily available' . . . Graham Clarke, 'The studio scene', *Kinematograph Weekly*, 17 December 1952, p. 18.

58 'the celebrity couple of the second features' . . . Stephen Chibnall and Brian McFarlane, *The British B Film*, p. 178.

59 'a stomach full of butterflies' . . . David Clayton, 'TV makes a star in five minutes', *Illustrated*, July 1953.

59 'Whatever happens from now on' . . . Clayton, 'TV makes a star in five minutes'.

60 four weeks to shoot . . . Clarke, 'The studio scene', p. 23.

61 'a competently made formula thriller' . . . British Film Institute, *Monthly Film Bulletin*, December 1953, p. 175.

61 'The red herrings' . . . Josh Billings, 'Reviews for showmen', *Kinematograph Weekly*, 22 October 1953, p. 18.

62 Cleveland actively discouraged her . . . Edward Bishop, 'Television topics', *Birmingham Weekly Post*, 15 April 1954.

62 'Jacqueline was sent' . . . 'She lost a job and won a husband', *TV Guide*, 27 April 1961, p. 2.

63 'Weeks later we met at a party' . . . Alvin Rakoff in conversation with Simon Guerrier and Thomas Guerrier, 2010.

63 'both agreed that the agent' . . . 'She lost a job and won a husband', *TV Guide*, 27 April 1961, p. 2.

63 'Has glamour' . . . Handwritten casting notes for *Golden Rain* (BBC WAC, Jacqueline Hill file 1).

64 'She is going through rather a tough time' . . . Letter, Kenneth Cleveland to Eric Fawcett, 6 April 1954 (BBC WAC, Jacqueline Hill file 1).

64 fashion competition in the *Daily Herald* . . . See various Fashion Contest features in the *Daily Herald*, 9–23 October 1953.

65 'do things properly' . . . Ann Davies in conversation with Simon Guerrier and Thomas Guerrier, 2010.

65   a suggestion from Michael Barry . . . Letter to Jacqueline Hill on behalf of Michael Barry, 13 October 1954 (BBC WAC, Jacqueline Hill file 1).

66   'Success-in-5-Minutes Girl' . . . James Green, 'Success-in-5-minutes girl comes back on TV', *Evening News*, 4 June 1955.

Chapter 7

67   'For what can television' . . . Alison Macleod, 'East End audience saw the humour', *Daily Worker*, 9 June 1955.

68   The spring of 1955 . . . See Jason Jacobs, *The Intimate Screen*, pp. 114, 115.

68   A telerecording was made . . . See contract for *The Legend of Pepito*, 18 May 1955; also letter from Angela Heathcote to Jacqueline Hill, 20 June 1955 (BBC WAC, Jacqueline Hill file 1).

68   a scheduling pattern . . . See *Radio Times*, 8 July 1955, p. 38, and Jacobs, *Intimate Screen*, p. 114.

69   'The BBC drama department' . . . Jacobs, *Intimate Screen*, pp. 114, 115.

69   'We were four days into rehearsals' . . . Quoted at <http://www.normanallan.com/Misc/Ted/nT%20ch%208.htm> (last accessed 30 June 2013).

70   'his fourth TV presentation' . . . 'Critics split over play by Ted Allan', *Montreal Gazette*, 7 June 1955.

71   'Never, until this week' . . . Alison Macleod, 'East End audience saw the humour', *Daily Worker*, 9 June 1955.

71   'Mexico on a plate' . . . Macleod, 'East End audience saw the humour'.

71   'the whole meaning of the play' . . . Macleod, 'East End audience saw the humour'.

72   'an unmistakable TV version' . . . Philip Purser, 'Showpieces: A tale of Pepito', *Daily Mail*, 4 June 1955.

72   'A little light relief' . . . Peter Black, 'Peter Black's Teleview', *Daily Mail*, 6 June 1955.

72 'a Tory television critic' . . . Macleod, 'East End audience saw the humour'.

73 'a range of stylistic features' . . . Jacobs, *Intimate Screen*, p. 117.

73 'The nearness of the television camera' . . . Jacobs, *Intimate Screen*, p. 119.

74 'On television Harry Towb' . . . Macleod, 'East End audience saw the humour'.

74 'small-screen television' . . . Cecil McGivern, 'The big problem', *BBC Quarterly* 5/3 (Autumn 1950), p. 147; quoted in Jacobs, *Intimate Screen*, p. 125.

75 'Jacqueline Hill, whose life was changed' . . . Green, 'Success-in-5-minutes girl'.

75 'watching with interest' . . . *Bournville Works Magazine*, June 1955, p. 208.

75 'Now that she was beginning' . . . Conversation with Alvin Rakoff, 2014.

76 'Dear Mr Allen' . . . Letter, Jacqueline Hill to Douglas Allen, 4 July 1955 (BBC WAC, Jacqueline Hill file 1).

76 'It was produced by Alvin Rakoff' . . . Letter, Jacqueline Hill to Barry Learoyd, 16 September 1955 (BBC WAC, Jacqueline Hill file 1).

Chapter 8

77 'I love an emotional scene' . . . 'She has to scream in American', *Evening Standard*, 10 November 1955, p. 6.

77 *The Times* ran a long piece . . . 'Television drama: "Live" or filmed beforehand?', *The Times*, 8 November 1955, p. 3. The technical innovations included so-called 'high definition' recording.

78 Tom Driberg interviewed Sir George Barnes . . . Tom Driberg, 'Sir George Barnes interviewed', *The New Statesman and Nation*, 12 November 1955, pp. 614 and 616.

78 'She was well suited to play American parts' . . . Alvin Rakoff in conversation with Simon Guerrier and Thomas Guerrier, 2010.

79 Screenwriter Stanley Mann . . . Mary Jane Miller, *Turn Up the Contrast: CBC Television Drama since 1952*, p. 197.

79 'That's why we all went' . . . See <http://www.normanallan.com/Misc/Ted/nT%20ch%209.htm> (last accessed 14 July 2019).

80 'probably our biggest draw' . . . Memo from Cecil Madden to Val Gielgud, 24 September 1954 (BBC WAC, Harry Green file: TV Art. Harry Green).

80 'I look forward to hearing' . . . Letter from Adrian Waller to Harry Green, 26 Sep 1955 (BBC WAC, Harry Green file: TV Art. Harry Green). Discussions between Green and the BBC about a possible long-term exclusive TV-only contract for him continued into December, but ultimately fell through. He continued to appear on both BBC and commercial television until his early death in 1958.

81 'endearing squashed lemon of a face' . . . Peter Currie, 'Thursday Play: *A Business of His Own*', *Radio Times*, 4 November 1955.

81 'lovable' . . . Philip Purser, 'Philip Purser's view . . .', *Daily Mail*, 11 November 1955.

81 'She has to scream in American' . . . 'She has to scream in American', *Evening Standard*. The 'two American girls', Alvin Rakoff suggests, may have been an invention of the reporter, although electoral registers do seem to show Jacqueline sharing accommodation with various flatmates during the early 1950s.

82 'Mr Green's own special merits' . . . Purser, 'Philip Purser's view . . .'.

82 'moving moments' . . . TV review, *Daily Mirror*, 11 November 1955.

82 'woefully unreal' . . . Maurice Richardson, 'Dizzy with infancy', *Observer*, 13 November 1955, p. 8.

83 'The whole thing is still in its infancy' . . . Richardson, 'Dizzy with infancy'.

Chapter 9

84   'The character of the woman Louise' . . . Peter Black, 'Peter Black's Teleview', *Daily Mail*, 28 December 1955.

84   Other highlights . . . M.E., 'Seven plays in two weeks', *The Stage*, 15 December 1955, p. 12.

85   a strong preference for ITV . . . David Kynaston, *Family Britain*, p. 607.

85   a *Radio Times* preview . . . Rowan Ayers, 'Three Empty Rooms: A new American play', *Radio Times*, 23 December 1955.

85   Raymond Williams has written . . . Raymond Williams, *Television: Technology and Cultural Form*, p. 54.

86   'to be used as an integral part' . . . JH contract for *Three Empty Rooms*, 1 December 1955 (BBC WAC, Jacqueline Hill file 1).

86   Filmed inserts in television plays . . . See Jason Jacobs, *The Intimate Screen*, pp. 131–6.

86   During the 1950s . . . See Jacobs, *Intimate Screen*, pp. 127–8.

87   'gambling at a card school' . . . Conversation with David Barry, 2014.

87   Following a two-day Christmas break . . . JH contract for *Three Empty Rooms*, 1 December 1955 (BBC WAC, Jacqueline Hill file 1).

88   Rehearsal that evening . . . Memo from Angela Heathcote at Tel. B.O. to JH, 4 January 1956 (BBC WAC, Jacqueline Hill file 1).

88   'British betrayers' . . . 'OUCH! – It's because they barred Hecht's daughter', *Daily Mail*, 21 December 1955, p. 5.

88   'this was not the sort of play to put on at holiday time' . . . Cyril Aynsley, 'Complaints? But this is a fine play', *Daily Express*, 28 December 1955, p. 3.

89   'screamed like someone from the Dark Ages' . . . 'TV play complaints', *Manchester Guardian*, 28 December 1955, p. 3.

89   'blood-curdling' . . . Alison Macleod, 'These are NOT the facts of life', *Daily Worker*, 30 December 1955, p. 2.

90   'This was a sensitive story' . . . Aynsley, 'Complaints?'

90   'The character of the woman Louise' . . . Peter Black, 'Peter Black's Teleview', *Daily Mail*, 28 December 1955.

91   'I understand you are casting' . . . Letter from JH to Alan Bromly, 7 February 1956 (BBC WAC, Jacqueline Hill file 1).

Chapter 10

92   'I always thought that' . . . Conversation with Alvin Rakoff, 2014.

92   'a sort of spoiled little rich girl' . . . Alvin Rakoff in conversation with Simon Guerrier and Thomas Guerrier, 2010; conversation with Alvin Rakoff, 2014.

93   'escapes sentence for attempted murder' . . . 'Televiews: The truth will out', *The Stage*, 19 April 1956.

93   'ingenious' . . . Philip Hope-Wallace, 'Critic on the hearth', *The Listener*, n.d. [April 1956], p. 477.

93   'too much of a madman's flytrap' . . . Maurice Richardson, 'The Argus Complex', *The Observer*, 22 April 1956, p. 10.

93   'Basil Sydney hated television' . . . Conversation with Alvin Rakoff, 2014.

94   'ITV's first rehearsal romance' . . . Philip Purser, 'Teleweekend', *Daily Mail*, 15 December 1956.

94   'I can remember talking with her about it' . . . Conversation with Alvin Rakoff, 2014.

95   'absolutely on the borderline of slum and respectability' . . . See <http://www.ladbrokeassociation.info/CLARENDONROAD.htm> (last accessed 14 July 2019).

95   'criminal class' . . . Keith Moore, 'Is this UK's most gentrified street?', <http://www.bbc.co.uk/news/magazine-18394017> (last accessed 14 July 2019).

95   Oswald Mosley's far-right Union Movement . . . Tom Vague, *Notting Hill History*, ch. 7, p. 10 <http://www.vaguerants.org.uk/wp-content/uploads/2010/06/timelinechap7.pdf> (last accessed March 2014).

96 'We were surrounded by tranquillity' . . . Conversation with
    Alvin Rakoff, 2014. The 'egg girl' may have been Fay Weldon,
    who famously wrote the slogan.

97 'Did Jackie mind?' . . . Conversation with Alvin Rakoff, 2014.

97 'I always thought that' . . . Conversation with Alvin Rakoff,
    2014.

Chapter 11

98 'I got a call from Jackie' . . . Alvin Rakoff in conversation with
    Simon Guerrier and Thomas Guerrier, 2010.

98 'more a melodrama of mood' . . . 'Plays of the week: *Requiem for
    a Heavyweight*', *Radio Times*, 29 March 1957.

99 'Jack ain't gonna show' . . . Conversation with Alvin Rakoff,
    2014.

99 'I had the devil's own job' . . . Alvin Rakoff in conversation with
    Simon Guerrier and Thomas Guerrier, 2010.

99 'She said, "Is he a heavyweight?"' . . . Alvin Rakoff in
    conversation with Simon Guerrier and Thomas Guerrier, 2010.

100 'So later that day' . . . Alvin Rakoff in conversation with Simon
    Guerrier and Thomas Guerrier, 2010.

101 'Rakoff was told over and over again' . . . Christopher Bray, *Sean
    Connery: The Measure of a Man*, p. 39.

101 'as surefooted as a cat' . . . Peter Black, 'Teleview: Here was a
    Summerskillian sermon', *Daily Mail*, 1 April 1957.

102 'The casting of Sean Connery' . . . 'Televiews: Twilight of a prize
    fighter', *The Stage*, 4 April 1957.

102 'The people of "Requiem for a Heavyweight"' . . . *The Listener*,
    'Drama: Rough stuff', n.d. [April 1957].

103 'Sean Connery owes his career' . . . Alvin Rakoff in conversation
    with Simon Guerrier and Thomas Guerrier, 2010.

103 'The springboard was always greater' . . . Conversation with
    Alvin Rakoff, 2014.

Chapter 12

104 'Jacqueline Hill, who plays the feminine lead' . . . 'Ursula Howells stars in Saturday serial', *The Stage*, March 1957.

104 'a tolerable Secret Service novel' . . . Daniel George, 'New novels', *The Spectator*, 3 August 1956, p. 27.

105 'wisecracking American nurse' . . . 'Ursula Howells stars', *The Stage*.

105 'an extraordinary woman' . . . Ian Dallas, '*Joyous Errand* – a modern quest', *The Listener*, n.d. [April 1957].

105 he had joined the BBC . . . 'Obituaries: Peter Lambert', *The Stage*, 13 July 2009.

106 '"Joyous Errand" began' . . . J. C. Trewin, *The Listener*, n.d. [April 1957].

106 'By now, doubtless' . . . J. C. Trewin, *The Listener*, n.d. [April 1957].

106 'Actor Peter Arne yesterday walked out' . . . '"Unhappy" actor quits TV show', *Daily Express*, 24 April 1957.

107 Again the problem was the script . . . 'Cook Harben walks out of Benny Hill Show', *Daily Express*, 26 April 1957.

107 Laurence Harvey dropped out . . . 'Now Harvey drops out of TV show', *Daily Express*, 27 April 1957.

107 'Dramatically last week' . . . A.M.D., 'Television commentary', *Glasgow Herald*, 18 May 1957.

108 'Since I last spoke to you' . . . Letter from JH to Gilchrist Calder, 31 August 1957 (BBC WAC, Jacqueline Hill file 1).

108 'Many thanks for your letter' . . . Letter from JH to Gilchrist Calder, 16 September 1957 (BBC WAC, Jacqueline Hill file 1).

Chapter 13

110 'She is described as a girl with a Transatlantic voice' . . . 'Voice two continents like', *Birmingham Mail*, 6 May 1958, p. 3.

110 an early brush with colour TV . . . Contract, *Her Affairs in Order*, 15 October 1957 (BBC WAC, Jacqueline Hill file 1).

111 in a form that was 'compatible' . . . Harold Bishop, 'Twenty-five years of BBC television'.

111 'a special programme was broadcast' . . . Bishop, 'Twenty-five years'.

112 Nagy was 'excellent' . . . 'Man on a diet', *The Stage*, 16 January 1958.

112 'a light-hearted piece about a young Welsh boy' . . . 'TV and Radio', *Birmingham Daily Post*, 30 May 1958.

113 it was evident to viewers . . . 'Harry Green dies after play', *Daily Mirror*, 31 May 1958.

113 'broke away from rehearsal at Granada headquarters' . . . 'Voice two continents like', *Birmingham Mail*, 6 May 1958, p. 3.

114 the *Birmingham Daily Post* called it 'enchanting' . . . 'Last night', *Birmingham Daily Post*, 7 August 1958, p. 17.

Chapter 14

115 'Sam Wanamaker as Ernie' . . . 'Radio and TV programmes', *Birmingham Daily Post*, 23 November 1959, p. 17.

116 'Because of their English accents' . . . Conversation with Alvin Rakoff, 2014.

116 'Repeatedly, he said it' . . . Conversation with Alvin Rakoff, 2014.

117 having 'returned from the "Velvet Alley" in New York' . . . 'BBC play on American television', *The Times*, n.d.

117 'where minutes are measured in dollars' . . . Rowan Ayers, 'The Velvet Alley', *Radio Times*, 20 November 1959.

118 'smooth with some nice angled shots and slick camera work' . . . Guy Taylor, 'Story of the knife-men', *The Stage and Television Today*, 26 November 1959.

118 'Two well-known producers' . . . Taylor, 'Story of the knife-men'.

119 'As the 60s differed from the 50s' . . . See John Finch, *Granada Television: The First Generation*, p. 51.

119 'brilliant' . . . 'exuberance' . . . Phil Diack, 'Let's be simply decent', *Daily Herald*, 23 November 1959; Mary Crozier, 'Television', *The Guardian*, 23 November 1959.

120 'No odious comparisons' . . . Peggy Lucas, 'Tele-drama comes into its own', *Daily Worker*, 24 November 1959.

120 'This was billed' . . . Maurice Richardson, 'Television and radio: Catharsis on the carpet', *The Observer*, 29 November 1959.

121 'another of those heartfelt American diatribes' . . . 'Drama: subjects and authors', *The Listener*, 26 November 1959.

121 'strong in a part that has been reflected by many' . . . Taylor, 'Story of the knife-men'.

121 'Jacqueline Hill came over strong' . . . 'Foreign television reviews', *Variety*, 2 December 1959.

122 'Nature of injury' . . . Accident report form, November 1959 (BBC WAC, Jacqueline Hill file 1).

122 'She was running towards him in elation' . . . Conversation with Alvin Rakoff, 2014.

122 As live broadcast crises go . . . See Gareth Rubin, 'Live TV drama is resurrected as Sky shrugs off lessons of history', *The Guardian*, 31 May 2009.

123 'It wasn't anything very serious' . . . Letter from JH to Bush Bailey, 3 December 1959 (BBC WAC, Jacqueline Hill file 1).

Chapter 15

124 'Usually I play sad parts' . . . 'She lost a job and won a husband', *TV Guide*, 27 April 1961, p. 2.

124 'ebulliently heartless' . . . Irving Wardle, 'Drama', *The Listener*, n.d. [May 1960].

125 'Jacqueline Hill stood out' . . . 'Foreign television reviews', *Variety*, n.d. [May 1960].

125 'new, specifically televisual form' . . . Janet Thumim, *Inventing Television Culture: Men, Women, and the Box*, p. 131.

126 'All the ages' . . . Kenneth Baily, 'Plays and players', *The Television Annual for 1961*, n.p.

126   Names on the initial list of contributing writers . . . Memo, 'BBC television drama: new writing', 26 August 1960 (BBC WAC, Drama Memos file T5/2, 239/3).

127   'the wonder and envy of television operators' . . . 'The BBC's new "factory"', *The Sphere*, 2 July 1960.

127   'Dressing rooms, wardrobe accommodation' . . . Lawrence Masidlover, 'Monument to confidence', *The Stage and Television Today*, 30 June 1960.

130   'serious and intelligent' . . . 'The Chopping Block', *The Times*, 24 October 1960.

130   'hen-pecked husband' . . . Anthony Cookman, Jnr, 'Drama: Dissension', *The Listener*, 27 October 1960.

131   'an extravagant story' . . . Mary Crozier, 'Television', *The Guardian*, 4 April 1961.

132   the BBC approached the London Cats' Protection League . . . 'Homeless kittens find fame', *Daily Mirror*, 3 April 1961; Alan Morris, 'Telegossip', *Newcastle Journal*, 17 February 1961.

132   'boring . . . it never really reached a dramatic climax' . . . 'An oh-so-boring drama', *The Stage and Television Today*, 6 April 1961.

133   'When the camera tries to make the flesh creep' . . . Richard Sear, 'Too creepy!', *Daily Mirror*, 4 April 1961.

133   'Though the plot was rather obvious' . . . Mary Crozier, 'Television', *The Guardian*, 4 April 1961.

133   'The obvious connection was with Eichmann' . . . Stewart Lane, 'Televiews', *Daily Worker*, 3 May 1961, p. 2.

133   *The Stage* agreed . . . 'A play that DIDN'T make its point at all well', *The Stage and Television Today*, 4 May 1961, p. 11.

134   '[W]e are getting an increasing number of plays' . . . G.B., 'TV and radio programmes', *Birmingham Daily Post*, 29 April 1961.

Chapter 16

136   'Her stock of four-letter words' . . . Conversation with Penny Francis, 2013.

137 'There is a singular pleasure' . . . Memo from Douglas Allen to Tel. Ed. Radio Times, 13 February 1962 (BBC WAC, *Six Proud Walkers* general file T5/2, 337/1).

137 'My dear Jackie' . . . Letter from Douglas Allen to JH, 29 January 1962 (BBC WAC, *Six Proud Walkers* general file T5/2, 337/1).

138 'with love' . . . Letter from Douglas Allen to JH, 1 February 1962 (BBC WAC, *Six Proud Walkers* general file T5/2, 337/1).

138 'She was a tremendous woman' . . . Conversation with Tony Britton, 2014.

139 'Douglas has got into a bit of a panic' . . . Memo from Dorothea Brooking to H.C.P. Tel., 7 April 1962 (BBC WAC, *Six Proud Walkers* general file T5/2, 337/1).

139 Wearing a fur coat . . . 'Diamond Jackie', *Daily Worker*, 10 March 1962, p. 2.

139 'neatness, pace' . . . 'Programme reviews: *The Six Proud Walkers*', *The Stage and Television Today*, 15 March 1962.

140 'Everybody took to Jackie' . . . Conversation with Penny Francis, 2013.

140 'Late at night, large quantities of whisky' . . . Conversation with Penny Francis, 2013.

141 The source material . . . Oliver Wake, '*Out of this World* (1962)'.

141 Story editor Irene Shubik . . . See Irene Shubik, *Play for Today: The Evolution of Television Drama*, p. 38.

142 'She was so bloody good' . . . Conversation with Tony Britton, 2014.

142 'breezy comedy and touches of genuine pathos' . . . Dick Richards, 'Waiting for the big break', *Daily Mirror*, 20 November 1964.

142 'one of those films you would think could not go wrong' . . . 'Film with an ingenious plot', *The Times*, 19 November 1964.

143 'the sort of performance that other actors daydream of' . . . Francis Fytton, 'Welcome to a new screen', *Birmingham Daily Post*, 21 November 1964.

144 'The women should wear normal summer clothes' ... *Maigret*, 'The Trap', BBC script by Margot Bennett, 1962.

144 'firm evidence of a style of acting' ... Richard Hewett, *The Changing Spaces of Television Acting*, pp. 91–2; © Manchester University Press, quoted with permission.

146 'a solid piece of drama' ... Richard Sear, 'Last night's TV', *Daily Mirror*, 9 October 1963.

146 'peculiarly attractive lingering quality' ... Anthea Hall, 'Television', *Newcastle Journal*, 12 October 1963.

147 'She was such a huge personality' ... Conversation with Penny Francis, 2013.

147 'I'm always writing to you about a change of agent' ... Letter from JH to Angela Heathcote, 21 January 1963 (BBC WAC: Jacqueline Hill file 2).

Chapter 17

148 'Don't let's waste time' ... Conversation with Penny Francis, 2013.

149 'the field of published science fiction' ... 'Science fiction report', 27 April 1962 (BBC WAC, Drama Memos file T5/2239/5).

150 'a frail old man lost in space and time' ... C. E. Webber, 'Background notes for "Dr. Who"' (BBC WAC, *Doctor Who* file T5/647/1).

150 'the ordinary people to whom extraordinary things happen' ... C. E. Webber, 'Background notes for "Dr. Who"'; '"Dr. Who": General notes on background and approach' (BBC WAC, *Doctor Who* file T5/638/1).

151 'I thought, I don't know whether Jacqueline will do this' ... From the documentary *Doctor Who: Origins* (2006).

151 Jacqueline gave her only long interview ... Interview with Jacqueline Hill, *Doctor Who Magazine*, October 1985.

152 'Jackie had a rather imposing personality' ... Quoted at <http://scifiandtvtalk.typepad.com/scifiandtvtalk/2011/01/sci-fi-

blast-from-the-past-carole-ann-ford-doctor-who.html> (last accessed 16 September 2018).

153 'In those tiny, tiny studios' . . . Interview with Jacqueline Hill, *Doctor Who Magazine*.

153 'We had lots of shared memories' . . . Interview with William Russell, *Radio Times*, 2010 <https://www.radiotimes.com/news/2010-11-01/interview-doctor-whos-william-russell/> (last accessed 14 July 2019).

153 'She was really remarkable' . . . This exchange between Russell and O'Brien is quoted from *Doctor Who: The Chase* (DVD), disc 1 commentary, 2010.

154 'We were lucky in having people like Waris' . . . Interview with Jacqueline Hill, *Doctor Who Magazine*.

155 'an imaginative and intelligently written story' . . . Marjorie Norris, 'Made for children but this will get a much wider audience', *The Stage and Television Today*, 5 December 1963.

156 'We were all absolutely fascinated with them' . . . Interview with Jacqueline Hill, *Doctor Who Magazine*.

157 'All I was actually told' . . . Interview with Jacqueline Hill, *Doctor Who Magazine*.

158 'in spite of the odds actually mines something emotional and true' . . . Robert Shearman and Toby Hadoke, *Running Through Corridors*, n.p.

158 'because I was given a bit more to do' . . . Interview with Jacqueline Hill, *Doctor Who Magazine*.

159 pleaded for a BBC photo call . . . Memo to Verity Lambert, 4 January 1965 (BBC WAC folder T5/1, 234/1, Doctor Who Serial M).

160 'soon lost its novelty value' . . . Interview with Jacqueline Hill, *Doctor Who Magazine*.

160 'She was terrifically kind' . . . From the documentary *Future Memories: The Making of 'The Dalek Invasion of Earth'* (2003).

161 'She was like a rock' . . . From *Doctor Who: The Chase* (DVD), disc 1 commentary, 2010.

162 'Everything that we wanted to do' . . . Interview with Jacqueline Hill, *Doctor Who Magazine*.

162 'As two of the cast leave of their own wish' . . . Marjorie Norris, 'Battle of the robots made this the best yet', *The Stage and Television Today*, 1965.

165 the 'moral centre' of the programme . . . Simon Guerrier, in the documentary *Last Stop White City* (2006).

166 'How easy was it to play the part' . . . Interview with Jacqueline Hill, *Doctor Who Magazine*.

166 'Jacqueline was quite determined' . . . See <http://missingepisodes.proboards.com/thread/6543/jacquline-hill> (last accessed March 2014).

Chapter 18

168 'I said to Jackie' . . . Interview with William Russell, *Radio Times*, 2010 <https://www.radiotimes.com/news/2010-11-01/interview-doctor-whos-william-russell/> (last accessed 14 July 2019).

169 'Stars of Dr WHO' . . . *Separate Tables* playbill, Leeds Grand Theatre, July 1965.

169 'Her Mrs Shankland is too young' . . . Desmond Pratt, 'Rattigan study of frustration', *The Yorkshire Post*, 21 July 1965.

169 'She and Alvin adopted' . . . Conversation with Penny Francis, 2013.

170 This cocooning stage was no indulgence . . . Thanks to Simon Guerrier for drawing my attention to this aspect of the adoption process.

170 'there were all sorts of reasons' . . . Conversation with Ann Davies, 2014.

171 'She adored her children' . . . Conversation with Sheila Hancock, 2013.

171 'The rest of life' . . . Correspondence with John D. Rakoff, 2019.

172 'It was such a big step for him' . . . Conversation with Marjorie Hill, 2013.

173 'I think because of what she had managed to get away from' . . . Conversation with Ann Davies, 2014.

174 'we were concerned that her age would be a factor' . . . Correspondence with Tim Combe, March 2013.

174 'I was at a conference about women' . . . 'Why these *Girlfriends* stand out in British TV', <https://www.bbc.co.uk/news/entertainment-arts-42225820> (last accessed 17 September 2018).

175 'eccentric interpretations' . . . '*Romeo* first of the 37', *The Stage and Television Today*, 9 November 1978, p. 19.

176 'Verona seemed to have been built on very level ground' . . . Clive James, 'Island of the stud tortoises', in *Clive James on Television*.

176 'It was not the happiest production' . . . Conversation with Alvin Rakoff, 2014.

176 'In those days, it was a bit of a death sentence' . . . Conversation with Sheila Hancock, 2013.

177 'Of course, television had moved on' . . . Interview with Jacqueline Hill, *Doctor Who Magazine*.

177 'One wonders what the actress made of this trip' . . . Gary Gillatt, 'Meglos', review for *Doctor Who Magazine* <https://gillatt.wordpress.com/2011/08/02/meglos/> (last accessed 17 September 2018).

178 'It's their first meeting' . . . Correspondence with Simon Guerrier, October 2018.

179 'tailored too tightly for the box' . . . Harry Thompson, 'Viewing review', *Newcastle Journal*, 12 July 1986, p. 9.

179 'beautifully acted' . . . Toby Manning, 'Your next box set: *Paradise Postponed*', *The Guardian*, 27 February 2014.

Chapter 19

181 'There are certain people' . . . Conversation with Sheila Hancock, 2013.

181 'Jackie had two bouts of cancer' . . . Ann Davies in conversation with Simon Guerrier and Thomas Guerrier, 2010.

182 'We didn't meet again' . . . Conversation with Sheila Hancock, 2013.

186 'I realised how ill she was' . . . Conversation with Penny Francis, 2013.

187 'She used to have to go' . . . Ann Davies in conversation with Simon Guerrier and Thomas Guerrier, 2010.

187 'I now know why' . . . Interview with William Russell, *Radio Times*, 2010 <https://www.radiotimes.com/news/2010-11-01/interview-doctor-whos-william-russell/> (last accessed 14 July 2019).

188 'She was determined to survive' . . . Alvin Rakoff in conversation with Simon Guerrier and Thomas Guerrier, 2010.

188 'The funny thing is' . . . Ann Davies in conversation with Simon Guerrier and Thomas Guerrier, 2010.

Chapter 20

190 'I didn't feel' . . . Conversation with Sheila Hancock, 2013.

191 'exist instead as shadows' . . . Jason Jacobs, *The Intimate Screen*, p. 14.

Index